MY REFUGE MY STRENGTH

MICHAEL YOUSSEF

HARVEST HOUSE PUBLISHERS
EUGENE, OREGON

Published in association with Don Gates of the literary agency, The Gates Group, www.thegatesgroup.com.

Cover design by Studio Gearbox
Cover images © by Oliver.zs / Shutterstock
Interior design by Aesthetic Soup

For bulk, special sales, or ministry purchases, please call 1-800-547-8979.
Email: CustomerService@hhpbooks.com

This logo is a federally registered trademark of the Hawkins Children's LLC. Harvest House Publishers, Inc., is the exclusive licensee of this trademark.

Select content is adapted from Michael Youssef, *I Long for You, O God* (Colorado Springs, CO: WaterBrook Press, 2004). Used with permission.

Select content is adapted from Michael Youssef, *Heal Me, O God* (Colorado Springs, CO: WaterBrook Press, 2003). Used with permission.

Select content is adapted from Michael Youssef, *I Praise You, O God* (Colorado Springs, CO: WaterBrook Press, 2002). Used with permission.

My Refuge, My Strength
Copyright © 2024 by Michael Youssef
Published by Harvest House Publishers
Eugene, Oregon 97408
www.harvesthousepublishers.com

ISBN 978-0-7369-8907-7 (Hardcover)
ISBN 978-0-7369-8908-4 (eBook)

Library of Congress Control Number: 2024931126

Printed in Colombia

24 25 26 27 28 29 30 31 32 / NI / 10 9 8 7 6 5 4 3 2 1

I will say of the LORD, "He is my refuge and my fortress, my God, in whom I trust."

PSALM 91:2

CONTENTS

PRAISING HIM AS MY REFUGE, MY STRENGTH

OUR EVER-PRESENT HELP

God is our refuge and strength, an ever-present help in trouble.
Therefore we will not fear, though the earth give way
and the mountains fall into the heart of the sea.

PSALM 46:1-2

A mid our troubles, when the world offers unsatisfying distractions and false spirituality, our hearts yearn for a sanctuary. We long for acceptance, love, safety, rest, and mercy. We search for shelter from the storms of our trials and watch for the light of hope to lead us.

We are created to respond this way, my friend, because in this life of difficulty *and* of blessing, our hearts hunger for the home they were made for—the presence of God. Join me for a journey…one that invites us to surrender our restlessness, move from discontent to contentment, and experience peace, healing, and a life of praising our Lord.

We get to know God's heart by reading His Word. We receive His comfort when we turn over our hurts to His care. And we experience His protection and power as we praise His name. My hope is that these devotions, biblical illustrations, Scriptures, and prayers will lead you to a profound intimacy with the Lord. As we embark on this journey together, I pray you will release your fears and worries and be filled with the abiding peace of Jesus. May you turn your heart and mind to the promise of God's ever-present help and enter the refuge of His strength and love all the days of your life.

Trust in him at all times, you people;
pour out your hearts to him,
for God is our refuge.

PSALM 62:7-8

LONGING FOR GOD'S PRESENCE

He satisfies the longing soul,
and fills the hungry soul with goodness.

PSALM 107:9 NKJV

How abundant are the good things that you have stored up
for those who fear you, that you bestow in the sight of all,
on those who take refuge in you.

PSALM 31:19

Are you convinced that if things were different, you would be happier and more at peace? Are you gaining less contentment from the things that consume most of your time and energy? Is there a steady background hum in your life—the dull hum of dissatisfaction?

This deep-seated discontent is not limited to those who are struggling with life's hurts and tragedies. In fact, a sense of dissatisfaction with life is often more pronounced among people who—from all outward appearances—seem to have it made. One's level of success does nothing to minimize the symptoms of discontent. The nagging inner voice continues to insist, *"There must be more."*

What lies behind our drive to find contentment? Some observers place the blame on materialism. But there is a far deeper explanation—a spiritual explanation for our lack of peace. God's Word makes it clear that our lack of peace and loss of satisfaction are spiritual issues.

As we study the Scriptures, we see that the loss of contentment can either lead us down paths cluttered with false promises of fulfillment, or it can bring us to a place of turning, where the journey takes on a redemptive quality. Our search for contentment can ultimately lead us to the heart of God—which is the only place where we will find rest and a place of belonging. It is the only place we will find the safety, identity, hope, healing, and strength we desire. It's the only place that will quiet our hearts and restore our souls.

This first part of our devotional journey will give you new insight into the heart of the only One who can quiet your discontent. As you delve into stories from God's Word, submit your restless spirit to Him and experience the satisfaction that comes from an intimate relationship with the One who died on the cross to give you peace.

1

FROM RESTLESS TO RESTORED

ave you felt it? The rumble of restlessness or the disruption of discontent in your spirit? Try as we might to find our own way to peace, an underlying lack of peace keeps many people in a state of unrest. Even if we aren't aware of it, our search for contentment produces an inner agitation, which is fed by the belief that we'll never be satisfied with where we are and that the answer is just beyond the next bend, the next job, the next relationship.

It might seem odd that we would study an ancient Bible story to find the explanation for our modern disease of discontent. But a spiritual cause is the only explanation for our restlessness. In the book of Genesis, restlessness first appears when Adam and Eve sin against God. The shame they feel after their disobedience brings an uneasiness and an unsettledness to their life. Those traits become more than simply feelings when God casts them out of the Garden of Eden.

Although Adam and Eve were allowed to remain near the garden, they constantly sensed their loss of intimacy with God. Their sin put distance between them and their Creator. And the same is true for us. Our sin moves us far from God and steals our contentment. To understand the implications of our sin nature, we must gain a clear picture of God's plan for humanity from beginning to end. In my view, this makes the first few chapters of the Bible critically important.

The Bible begins with creation. As God created matter out of nothing, He set aside a special place, Eden, where He fellowshipped with Adam and then with Eve. In this incredibly beautiful garden, Adam and Eve enjoyed unhindered communion with God.

But they forfeited their contentment and were banished from the garden when they disobeyed God and ate from the forbidden tree. This set in motion an ongoing quest to regain the peace that had been forfeited.

Since then, men and women throughout the ages have sought an end to their restlessness. In his memoir, *Confessions*, written in AD 400, Augustine recounts how he overcame his lustful pursuits and found peace. In a moment of truth, he realized that there is only one solution. Explaining humankind's inborn desire to seek God and to praise Him, Augustine wrote, "You have made us for Yourself, and our hearts are restless until they find their rest in You."*

Here it is in a nutshell: The place of ultimate rest is found nowhere else but in intimate relationship with the Lord. We are made in the image and likeness of our heavenly Father, and we all share an abiding need to be in close communion with Him.

Much happens after Adam and Eve leave the garden. And the journey through Scripture reveals not only the cause of our restlessness, but it also leads us to the perfect solution found at the end of the Bible and in another garden described in Revelation as the New Jerusalem, a magnificent garden city that will come down from heaven. God wants to restore us to a place of contentment in His love and grace, so He provides a place of peace, rest, and belonging where our search for contentment comes to an end.

Until our time in heaven, we can experience peace here and now because Christ, in a garden experience between Genesis and Revelation—the Garden of Gethsemane—agreed to the Father's will that He pay the penalty for the sins of all who would willingly receive Him as their Savior.

---

* Augustine, *Confessions* (New York: Oxford University Press, 1998), 1.

Friend, God wants to refresh our souls—to replace anxiety with peace, to give us rest in place of weariness, to provide a place of belonging that will quiet our restlessness once and for all. Day by day, we can trust Jesus to keep leading us to His calm waters and a grace that redeems.

The LORD bless you
    and keep you;
the LORD make his face shine on you
    and be gracious to you;
the LORD turn his face toward you
    and give you peace.

NUMBERS 6:24-26

Lord, as I begin this devotional journey, use my restlessness to draw me close to You. Search my heart and reveal to me which longings may hold me back from embracing Your truths or walking in the path You have set for me.

As I experience this journey toward the New Jerusalem, may I believe and proclaim the good news of Calvary. May I live in the grace and salvation You alone can provide. In Your Word, Lord, You promise that when I seek You, I will find You. Help me to trust that You are the only source of true contentment. I call out to You and seek You for my restoration. You turn to me with Your grace, peace, and love, and You refresh my spirit. The blessings of relationship with You impact my today and my eternity. I'm so grateful I belong to You. Amen.

2

THE PEACE OF PARADISE

When God created Adam and Eve, they had perfect contentment. Why wouldn't they? They were in paradise, and they had communion with their Creator. As we look at our world, circumstances, and the restlessness of sin and then consider what they had in Eden, the contrast between our lack of contentment and the true peace God desires for His creation is shocking.

We can praise God today, friend, because He still has a plan for our peace. Wander these aspects of God's care in the first garden and discover how the merciful Lord continues to provide what we need for contentment until the day we regain residency in eternal paradise with Him.

Exquisite beauty. As God created every part of the universe, He pronounced it "good." But He unleashed the full extent of His creative power when He designed a garden home for Adam and Eve. For their enjoyment, He poured out beauty beyond comprehension.

Our word "paradise" comes from the Persian word *pardes* that refers to a garden or enclosed park. The same word also connotes a place of peace and protection—exactly what the Garden of Eden was designed to provide. Take time to consider how you personally experience beauty and the goodness of the Lord right now.

Abundant provision. The beauty of the Garden of Eden also was functional.

The trees were not only pleasing to the eye but also good for food. As part of God's plan of provision, He assigned Adam the job of maintaining the garden.

Before the Fall, Adam and Eve didn't just lounge around all day—they had work to do. "The LORD God took the man and put him in the Garden of Eden to work it and take care of it" (Genesis 2:15). Adam and Eve had important work to do, but they were working inside the garden, in God's presence, and that made all the difference. They found fulfillment in the satisfying work God gave them. How is God providing for your basic needs as well as assigning work for you to do for His glory? Spend time in prayer and praise for the abundance in your life.

Complete protection. God sheltered Adam and Eve, guarding them from all danger. Within the garden's walls, Adam and Eve lived in an atmosphere of sweet harmony with each other and with God. While they enjoyed the protection in the garden, they fell for the serpent's deception and exposed themselves to danger. In the middle of the garden, God placed a special tree called the Tree of the Knowledge of Good and Evil, and God instructed Adam and Eve not to eat the fruit of this tree. Their choice to eat the forbidden fruit took them out from under God's complete protection.

Praise the Lord that this is not the end of the story for God's children. Many years later, Jesus's perfect obedience led Him from the Garden of Gethsemane to the cross, making it possible for His followers to be forgiven of their sins and to once again be under His protection for eternity.

In the Garden of Eden, the first man rebelled against God. But in the Garden of Gethsemane, Jesus, the perfect God-man, agreed to obey His Father and sacrifice Himself on the cross. God revealed His perfect plan to give us victory over the sin that was born in the Garden of Eden and to reveal beauty, provide for us, protect us, and fellowship with us as we surrender to Him and live in His wisdom.

Consider today whether you are kneeling at the foot of the tree of temptation or at the tree of Calvary. It's your surrender at the cross that leads to your hope in heaven, your hope in a return to paradise, and the assurance that your peace and contentment will be found in right relationship with God in the garden of your heart today.

⟋⟍

Blessed are those who find wisdom,
    those who gain understanding...
Long life is in her right hand;
    In her left hand are riches and honor.
Her ways are pleasant ways,
    And all her paths are peace.
She is a tree of life to those who take hold of her;
    those who hold her fast will be blessed.

PROVERBS 3:13, 16-18

Father God, give me strength to turn from choices that are leading me away from the paradise of Your love and provision. Even though Adam and Eve had to leave Eden, You continue to rescue the godly and bless them with beauty, provision, and protection. I pray to surrender my will to Your own and to kneel at the cross with a sincere and open heart. May my obedience in word and action reflect my devotion.

Thank You for Your everlasting love and protection. I know You desire to have a personal relationship with me. Show me how I can draw closer to You through Your Word. I want to walk in Your power with an obedient heart, mind, and spirit. Give me the courage and wisdom to have a Gethsemane heart of conviction and experience Your victory and a return to paradise to spend my eternity with You. Amen.

3

TIRED OF WANDERING

As soon as sin enters our lives, it influences and impacts more than one moment, one thought, one decision. It seeps into every aspect of life, including our families and our trust in God.

Adam and Eve regretted the break in their relationship with God. They owned up to their sin of surrendering to temptation in Eden, but their shame, grief, and regret did not protect their son Cain from falling into sin. And it was a grave, heartbreaking sin.

Despite his parents' conscientious teaching, Cain's disobedience far surpassed that of Adam and Eve. Cain's anger led to the murder of his brother Abel.

The sin grew in his heart because he was angry that God accepted Abel's offering while rejecting his own. Cain brought an offering to the Lord from his harvest. Abel also brought an offering, the firstborn from his flock. The brothers' offerings were consistent with their occupations: Cain tilled the ground and Abel raised sheep. Outwardly, both brothers seemed to be performing a righteous act. But Cain wanted to approach God on his own terms.

The Bible doesn't specify how either brother knew whether God accepted or rejected his offering, but it's clear they understood the outcome: "The LORD looked with favor on Abel and his offering, but on Cain and his offering he did not look with favor. So Cain was very angry, and his face was downcast"

(Genesis 4:4-5). We can imagine the anger and pride brewing in his heart. God knew what was happening inside Cain. And He could have left him to his anger right then, but God didn't want Cain to fail and surrender to sin. So He issued a stern warning, telling Cain that sin was lying in wait for him. God also offered mercy, making it clear that if Cain did what was right, he would be accepted (see Genesis 4:6).

Cain refused to heed God's warning. Instead, he enticed his younger brother into a field where he beat him to death. Unlike Adam and Eve, who first tried to make excuses for their sin in the garden, Cain denied his sin. When God confronted him, Cain said he knew nothing about his brother's murder. As punishment, Cain had to leave the land of Eden and became "a restless wanderer on the earth" (Genesis 4:12).

When we revisit this well-known story, we clearly see the trail of bad choices made by Cain. His disobedience is glaring. His complete denial of his sin is shocking. You might think, *I would never commit such a sin!* It's true you're not likely to murder your sibling, but if you examine your life, you might see a time when you made a series of decisions that led you to be ruled by sin instead of obedience to God. And maybe recently you avoided your opportunity to confess a sin. Instead, you chose to ignore it, deny it, hide it under a series of good deeds, or conveniently omit it from your time of prayer with your heavenly Father.

People today are running from God. Perhaps they are not even aware they are wandering spiritually. But running from God will never alleviate the guilt of sin. Only one remedy exists, and that is found in facing up to our shortcomings. The way to deal with sin and guilt is through confession and repentance.

Like Cain, you and I are given the opportunity to do what is right and stay in God's presence. Are you facing a challenge? A temptation? Pause and dwell on God's Word before choices are made that could leave you wandering, running, and even hiding from the Lord. Whether you feel pulled toward sin by pride or by the tension of difficulties, stop to seek God. In His mercy, He waits for you. Go to your Father. He welcomes you and your willing heart.

Have mercy on me, O God,
>according to your unfailing love;
according to your great compassion
>blot out my transgressions.

PSALM 51:1

Lord, there have been times when I have run from You. I have hidden from You because of my sin and guilt. But I am tired of living apart from Your love and protection. You have pointed out my transgressions and the areas in my life where I have walked to the edge of what is right and either entertained or given in to sin.

Help me to pause and pray when I encounter temptation or strong emotions that can cloud my focus on what is right. I will listen to the words You place on my heart and those You have given to me in Scripture. I believe You are eager to receive me and accept my sincere offering of prayer and this life I live. I pray for the wisdom to stop wandering aimlessly and, instead, run with intention toward Your unfailing love. Amen.

4

AT HOME IN GOD'S PRESENCE

Most believers can probably look back on a time when they veered away from a particular path God was calling them to walk with His guidance. Maybe the choice was related to a job or a relationship. Maybe it was a moral or spiritual dilemma. Some people of faith may take a short detour before coming to their senses and getting back on course in time to avoid doing grave damage. But there are many who stay on the false trail far too long, and it isn't until catastrophe strikes that they look behind them with regret at all the chaos and debris in their wake and get on their knees to repent.

No matter how our path of sin began or where we are along the detour, when we seek God, our refuge and strength, we are redeemed. But the one who continues to wreak havoc and who refuses to turn back to God and surrender becomes hardened, distant from the voice of the Lord, and entrenched in his way.

Cain was such a man. He was given a chance to repent, but he chose instead to reject God's mercy. He tried to run from God and built his own city, and each generation of his descendants living in that city achieved a new level of wickedness. The city was filled with lonely, hard, arrogant, self-seeking people. This is because choosing a self-directed life instead of obedience to God always leads to loneliness and isolation.

Contrast this with the Garden of Eden. Fear and anxiety didn't exist there because God was Adam and Eve's Protector. There was no possibility of economic collapse because God was their Provider. God intended for His people to live in this unspoiled, safe environment, but man chose to wander from God and build a city.

In a large city you can find masses of people, though many feel a deep sense of loneliness. Uncomfortable being alone, people tend to gather in groups and yet remain disconnected and full of discontent. Most people concentrate on their own concerns, hardly think of others, and fail at intimacy. Even husbands and wives can feel like strangers. Sometimes we are too afraid to look in our own hearts, let alone share our thoughts and feelings with another person. Being intimate means opening up to one another and being vulnerable, and that's a risk many of us are not willing to take.

This is not the way God meant for us to live. He designed us to need one another. In the garden, Adam and Eve fellowshipped with God, enjoying each other's company and sharing the wonder of their environment.

Cain did just the opposite as he deliberately put distance between himself and God. If we follow Cain's example, seeking refuge apart from the presence of God, we will never find peace. The peace we yearn for can be found only in the garden of God's grace.

Which direction have you been going in lately? Are you journeying away from or toward the Protector and Provider? The condition of your heart and mind will let you know. If your first thoughts and first worries are about you or concerns of the world, chances are you have gone some distance from the presence of Jesus. If your thoughts turn quickly to prayer and your inclination is to release the burden of your fears and needs to Jesus, then your heart is drawing near to Him.

The refuge of God's presence awaits. It does not need to be the place you crawl back to after the world has broken you down. This refuge is meant to be your home base where you enjoy His company, draw from His strength, and are empowered for all that is required of you as you make your way *with* Him in this world.

———

Trust in the LORD with all your heart
    and lean not on your own understanding;
 in all your ways submit to him,
    and he will make your paths straight.

PROVERBS 3:5-6

No place of refuge apart from You, Lord, will satisfy my restless heart. No other person, relationship, or situation will bring lasting peace into my life. Help me walk away from the false promises of the "city of man." I want my home, my refuge, to be in Your presence so I will remain under Your protection and provision all of my days.

Show me what is in my heart that leads me away from intimacy with You. Show me how to put my trust in who You say You are and who You say I am. Reveal to me the areas of my life that displease You so that I may repent and be restored to fellowship with You. It is a privilege to be known fully by You, and it is a blessing—and a great relief—to trust Your understanding and direction for my life. Amen.

5

THE HOPE OF EDEN

It's been a long time since Eden was home for God's children. In fact, it's been so long that the idea of a place without violence, selfishness, pain, anger, and destruction seems impossible, doesn't it? After Adam and Eve had to leave paradise, they still had a strong memory of what it was like to live in constant fellowship with their Creator. Imagine their sense of loss, regret, and separation as they realized life would never be the same.

While some descendants strove to repair intimacy with God, others were drawn to the offerings of the city of man, where pride and arrogance ruled and there was no accountability to anyone, least of all God. In such an amoral climate, violence runs rampant and justice is perverted. The freedom found in a "to each his own" culture fosters an entitlement to harm others—a license to destroy to get what one wants regardless of who or what is in the way.

Such heartlessness is echoed in a song by the vengeful Lamech. With a demeanor of invincibility and a desire to build his power and image, he boasts of inflicting violence on his enemies: "Adah and Zillah, listen to me; wives of Lamech, hear my words. I have killed a man for wounding me, a young man for injuring me. If Cain is avenged seven times, then Lamech seventy-seven times" (Genesis 4:23-24).

In the Hebrew language, these words come across as defiance against God.

Lamech might as well have been saying, "God does not run the world according to my preferences, so I have decided to take things into my own hands."

Lamech's boasting would not sound unusual today in a culture that tries to overthrow all vestiges of authority—especially God's authority. One doesn't even have to seek the company of those who spew defiance to be exposed to harmful rhetoric. It's all over social media and the places we gather our information.

And it never goes unnoticed by the Lord. That's exactly what we see in Scripture:

> The LORD saw how great the wickedness of the human race had become on the earth, and that every inclination of the thoughts of the human heart was only evil all the time. The LORD regretted that he had made human beings on the earth, and his heart was deeply troubled. So the LORD said, "I will wipe from the face of the earth the human race I have created—and with them the animals, the birds and the creatures that move along the ground—for I regret that I have made them" (Genesis 6:5-7).

What a shocking proclamation—the annihilation of all living beings! Yet God is not without mercy. The very next verse says, "But Noah found favor in the eyes of the LORD" (Genesis 6:8).

We're familiar with the story of Noah's building an ark and loading it with his family and two of every animal. While God brought judgment on human wickedness, He also preserved a faithful remnant and even made gracious provision for the animal kingdom. His wrath turned to a merciful act to save His creation.

We don't have personal memories of the beauty, safety, and peace of Eden… or of what the floodwaters destroyed, but God's Word reminds us of His mercy *and* His might. And our present longing for God's refuge reminds us to keep looking to God alone as our Guide, our Lord, and our Savior.

Consider how you find favor with the Lord. Are you faithful? Do you express His mercy and love to others even when they don't deserve unconditional love? Step into your day with God's heart for those you encounter and for your own circumstance. You may not be in Eden, but you can hold on to the hope God had for His children in the beginning and the hope He still has for you as your Provider and Lord.

I will remember my covenant between me and you and all living creatures of every kind. Never again will the waters become a flood to destroy all life.

Genesis 9:15

Lord, forgive me for the times I have boasted about living life on my terms and filling my longings with things of the world. It's clear to me that there is no peace in the "city of man." There is only eternal restlessness there. I want the desires of my heart to reflect those You have for me, and I want to be like Noah, faithfully walking with You.

I'm grateful that my longing leads to Your presence. You guide me away from my restless pursuits and bring me to a place of contentment and purpose. You don't ask that I earn these blessings. You ask only that I trust You as the source for them. Fill me with Your mercy and Your might so I can confidently share about Your love and find favor in Your eyes. I will praise Your name all my days from now to eternity. Amen.

6

BUILDING FOR GLORY OR GOD

W hat you build with your time, energy, and resources reflects your priorities as well as the state of your spirit. Is the business, reputation, house, legacy, family, or life you are constructing something worthy of the blessings from God you are using to create it?

While we spend the first part of this devotional journey together looking at some examples in Scripture of how man avoided or pursued relationship with God, several stories shine a light on how man tries to replace God or build legacies apart from God. One of the most familiar examples is the Tower of Babel.

Many people know the story of God's confusing the languages at the Tower of Babel, but what is less familiar is the rebellion that motivated the tower's construction. The Bible tells us that Nimrod was a proud and powerful king who couldn't comprehend serving anyone. He attempted to prove that he had no need of God by devoting his life to building a civilization in opposition to God's authority. He built the famed Tower of Babel as a symbol of human effort in trying to find contentment apart from God.

Nimrod's tower was, in many ways, the next step in a progression of human rebellion against God. Adam and Eve sinned but settled near the Garden of Eden, remaining close to God's presence. Cain murdered his brother and then ran from God, settling in the land of Nod. Nimrod took this progression of sin several steps further, establishing an entire civilization in opposition to God. His desire was for the top of the tower to reach the heavens for the worship of the heavenly bodies—not the Maker of those heavens.

It was from Babylon that astrology—the belief that the stars and planets influence human affairs and events on earth—was passed on to the entire world. That belief continued on. After 400 years of slavery in Egypt, even the Hebrews had begun to practice astrology. When the Lord brought them out of Egypt, He warned them against worshiping the stars (see Deuteronomy 18:9-13).

Although Nimrod's tower was constructed in ancient times, it might surprise you to know there is a Babylonian revival in our own time. This pagan revival has fostered a host of popular practices, including tarot cards, horoscopes, and psychic hotlines. The price tag of this growing interest in pagan spirituality is astronomical in both its financial and spiritual impact, as many people have destroyed their lives by acting on advice from psychics and shamans. If they had sought God's counsel instead, they could have been spared untold regret.

Every disease and sickness, every heartache and pain, is the result of original sin. Many people reject Christ's sacrifice that can bring salvation, choosing instead to try to conquer sin's consequences on their own terms. The arrogance that led Nimrod to construct the tower is no different than the arrogance that continues to rule those who refuse God's authority. Many believe that given enough money and time, we can do anything. We place our trust in science and supercomputers. Technology has become our god. When people claim their success came only from their effort, genius, or authority, they have abandoned the knowledge of God and dependence on Him.

Today, take a moment to consider what you are building to be certain it is not more about your desire for recognition and influence than it is about following and praising God. We can innocently create something that initially serves others and is pleasing to God, but, in time, as momentum or power builds, the original intention fades.

Friend, when God gives you the desires of your heart, always remember the Who behind your heart, its desire, and the fulfillment of that desire. Only then will whatever you are building endure as a testament of your faithfulness and His.

Commit to the LORD whatever you do,
    and he will establish your plans.

PROVERBS 16:3

Father, You know my heart and my mind. Is there anything I am building with a hidden desire to make a name for myself rather than to glorify Your name? Show me where I have shifted the focus from You to me, from Your promises to my popularity. When I serve and minister to others, give me a humble heart. When I create, may I praise You for ideas and for the privilege of cocreating with You.

If my investment of money, attention, abilities, and effort is for personal gain, lift the veil of that pride and redirect my focus so I am tender toward the priorities and people You want under my care. Lead me, Lord. May I build a tower above my human limits so in all that I do, I point to You and Your strength alone. You are my lasting foundation. Amen.

7

TURNING FROM IDOLS

When discontent comes upon us, the temptation can be great to seek answers from our immediate circle of peers, coworkers, thought leaders, and media influencers. We can look at Nimrod and clearly see his defiance. It's much harder to notice the times we are acting in a similar way and either becoming our own mini god or trusting our version of idols for direction.

Unless we have a strong, faithful habit of turning to the Lord each day for wisdom, going to Him with our plans and ambitions may not be our first instinct. Or even our last. That leaves a lot of room for input not of God to guide our decisions, choices, and actions.

Notice Satan's modus operandi. After he was thrown out of heaven, Satan deceived Adam and Eve into doubting God and managed to get them thrown out of the garden. Then Satan deceived Cain into worshipping in his own way rather than God's way, which led to Abel's murder and ultimately to the massive destruction of life by the flood. Then Satan deceived Ham's descendants into worshipping the zodiac—actually the worship of demons—thereby causing their destruction.

Satan always sows deception and confusion. He convinces people to take a gift and turn it into an idol. The Babylonians used their innate desire for self-preservation to build a monument to glorify themselves. They turned

God's gift of self-protection into an idol of self-worship. When people don't worship God, they embrace false gods, intentionally or not.

Idol worship happens today, often without our realizing it. The most dominant among our idols is the god of self. Our resources, our energy, our time—our complete focus is on the self. Slick politicians make campaign speeches that cater to the powerful god of self. The advertising industry dedicates itself to feeding the god of self.

Focusing on ourselves and our abilities—whether self-esteem or self-actualization—will produce the opposite of the contentment that we long for because our perspective is limited and our aim falls short of God's purpose. For example, humanity uses modern technology to build great buildings, and these towering edifices engender great pride. When you stand on the ground looking up at the Sears Tower, it literally makes you dizzy. But when you fly above that same skyscraper, it looks insignificant. From God's perspective, all of humanity's achievements amount to nothing more than a pimple on the face of the planet.

In our discontented pursuit of a "better" self, we're not that different from the Babylonians. When the Babylonian council assembled to defy God and try to steal His glory, God assembled His own council. The divine meeting I'm referring to is described in Genesis 11:6-7: "The Lord said, 'If as one people speaking the same language they have begun to do this, then nothing they plan to do will be impossible for them. Come, let us go down and confuse their language so they will not understand each other.'"

The council of the Holy Trinity caused a massive human communication problem that prevented the tower from being completed. God's judgment always prevails, and those who continue to worship the god of self will always be frustrated and sometimes even destroyed.

Turning your focus to God will lead you away from the distractions and lure of idols, including self. You can protect your heart and move out of discontent by spending time with the Lord and in His Word. In your journey as a Christian, you have probably heard this advice many times. Maybe it seems too simple to be true. But contentment, purpose, and peace emerge when you are immersed in God's wisdom, stand firm in His truth, and open your life to His guidance.

Our earthly idols don't care about our fate, but God, our Maker, does. Allow your longings to be sated by His presence and unconditional, never-changing love.

You make known to me the path of life;
    you will fill me with joy in your presence,
    with eternal pleasures at your right hand.

PSALM 16:11

Lord, have I allowed anything to become an idol in my life? If so, I pray You would reveal it to me now. I know You warn against idolatry because of Your love for me. You want what is best for me, and that best is to glorify You with all of my being.

I often try to do things my own way and in my own strength without asking for Your help or Your plan. Help me to avoid the temptation to rely on my limited abilities and vision. And protect me from looking to the world's deceptive practices for knowledge. Instead, turn my heart toward the truth of Your Word and my feet toward the good works You have prepared for me. With gratitude I move from discontent to peace and joy when I trust Your mercy, wisdom, and purpose. Amen.

8

RUNNING TO GOD

Have you experienced a dark valley in your life journey? Maybe you are struggling with the weight of a weary spirit and mind today, and this message comes when you need it most. While many men and women of the Bible sought earthly contentment apart from God, there were others whose unsettled lives and times of darkness ultimately drove them into the Lord's presence. Their wandering led them in the opposite direction of their ancestors. They ran to God instead of away from Him.

David, in all the upheaval of his life, was constantly running to God. In all his candid questions and passionate expressions of vulnerability, we don't sense that David ever lost faith in God's power to make things right. What may surprise you is that David, a man of faith, appeared to have several bouts with what modern psychologists would label depression.

Christians often are ashamed to admit to dark periods of despair and depressive illnesses. The life of David, however, teaches us that possibly every person, even those who trust God, at some point enters a dark valley. In fact, almost anyone who responds to the call of God will one day face doubts and questions, difficulties and trials, that will lead him or her through the door of depression. Jeremiah was known as the "weeping prophet" because he anguished over the sins of God's people and the judgment he saw coming as a result of their disobedience. More than once he withdrew in defeat and asked God why he had even been born.

Like Jeremiah and other dedicated servants of God, David experienced a similar bout of depression. "You, God, are my God, earnestly I seek you; I thirst for you, my whole being longs for you, in a dry and parched land where there is no water" (Psalm 63:1). His longing for God, even in the pit of despair, is a vivid demonstration of a soul's response to difficult times. If we are willing, we can turn our despair into a passionate pursuit of God. That's when the search for peace—and deliverance from the dark valley—brings us back to God's heart.

When our spirits are dry and the landscape of our life is parched, we may not initially be able to summon that hunger for God. Difficult circumstances and losses may leave you in shock or usher you into a season of dismay and disappointment. But God does not disappoint. And with each small step you take to be in His presence and notice His grace and care, that hunger can be stirred. The thirst for Him can be strong. And the desire for the life He has for you can be renewed.

God will not leave us in a spiritual state of lack as we pursue His leading. He fills and satisfies us. When the Israelites were desperate for nourishment and sustenance as they wandered the desert, God sent manna afresh each day to be sure they had what their bodies needed to continue. They complained that the manna spoiled when they tried to save it. Instead of storing it up, they had to trust that the Lord would rain down His daily provision every day. God was providing for their physical need to show them a spiritual truth: They needed Him and could not do the journey alone.

Begin your journey of trust with the Lord. In your heartache, lack, loss, or hardship, watch for daily provision from Him. In your weariness, you can rely on Him to faithfully feed your spirit. He will replace your ache of hunger with satisfying fulfillment. He will quench your thirst for wellness with His living water. Run to the heart of God and receive the love that will sate your daily need with eternal provision. He will accompany you through the dark valley and into the light of assurance and hope.

He humbled you, causing you to hunger and then feeding you with manna, which neither you nor your ancestors had known, to teach you that man does not live on bread alone but on every word that comes from the mouth of the Lord.

Deuteronomy 8:3

Heavenly Father, I confess that at times I have been overwhelmed with feelings of despair. But I draw hope from the example of Your servant David, who continued to seek You even in the darkest valley. When I have been so distraught that I cannot sense You are near, You stir within me a hunger for righteousness and a thirst for Your love. You meet me there…in the dark and in the longing. You never leave me in my wilderness without direction or provision.

As I take in Your Word and Your promises as truth and sustenance, their abundance overflows into my life, mindset, and capacity to hope. Now I rise in the morning and lie down at night with gratitude because I know I have not been forgotten by You. My tears now reap songs of joy because without fail You provide the manna this weary spirit needs. Amen.

9

COME TO THE WATER

People aren't always willing to receive the help they need. I confess to moments of digging in my heels and declining help during a rough part of my journey. Can you relate to this? Have you faced a looming obstacle so large you knew you would need help to overcome it, and yet you rebuffed offers of assistance from friends, coworkers, or your spouse? From God?

If you have ever watched a loved one refusing help, even when their situation is dire, then you know what God must feel like each time one of His children turns from His salvation, His grace, His healing, His offer of replenishment.

Psalm 42 is a beautifully poetic description of spiritual need, showing that the answer to our restlessness is a driving thirst for God: "As the deer pants for streams of water, so my soul pants for you, my God" (Psalm 42:1). In the moment of our deepest discouragement, relief comes only when we thirst for God.

The writer of Psalm 42 does not offer platitudes. He cuts through the pat answers and tells us that the only spring of water that will satisfy our desperate need is the Living Water. I can picture David observing an exhausted deer—spent, feverish, and desperate for water—finally reaching the edge of a stream.

David himself was desperate as he considered the threats of his murderous son Absalom. For David, only the fountain of God could satisfy his spiritual thirst and alleviate his emotional fever.

That's what we all need to be: thirsting for God and not the trappings of religion. For example, we need to ask ourselves: Are we going to church to hear a compelling sermon or beautiful music? Are we going for programs and social activities? Or are we going to meet God—our only source of refreshment and life?

Are we praying for self-advancement and to receive things of the world we hope will satisfy our gnawing, spiritual ache? Or are we kneeling to sip from the streams of Living Water and receive what God alone has for us? Are we humbling our hearts before God and asking that His will be done?

When we seek contentment in anything but God, we miss the first, most important source for restoration: the Living Water. Only a burning thirst for God will bring satisfaction. And while it would be great if we had that thirst all the time to bring us again and again to those waters, it often takes the exact hardship we are cursing in order for us to be ready to receive the ever-flowing help of the Lord.

Even the most stubborn among us will likely reach the point when we are so tired, worn, or worried that we're willing to let our guards down and receive. All David could do was weep tears of pain, exhaustion, grief, and despair. There is a blessed release in tears. If we refuse tears, we are refusing a God-ordained channel of restoration. David knew he needed God desperately. There was nowhere else to turn. There was no help coming from another source. He also knew from his history with the Lord that God was faithful.

When we are connected to Jesus, we have a balm in times of suffering. His name is a healing ointment that soothes our spirits. There are different seasons in life—times of weeping and mourning and times of laughter and dancing. If you are going through a season of sorrow, keep in mind that as David poured out his soul to the Lord, he reclaimed his joy.

And if you are in a time of dancing, don't wait until you are without reserves to go to the source for spiritual refreshment. Be with Jesus every day. His steady stream of grace will satisfy, heal, and prepare you for the purposes He has for you.

My soul thirsts for God, for the living God.
When can I go and meet with God?
My tears have been my food
day and night,
while people say to me all day long,
"Where is your God?"

PSALM 42:2-3

Lord, it's hard to admit to needing help and even harder to accept it at times. But I come to You today as an empty vessel ready to be filled with Your strength. I need Your help in my weariness. I long for Your healing presence and Your peace to return to my life.

I am sorry for the times I have joined with others who have asked "Where is God? Where is He in my pain and suffering?" I know You are with me and have waited with compassion and patience for me to accept the help You offer. Today I come to You as the Living Water. I take in Your refreshment and exchange my sorrows for the comfort of Your Holy Spirit. May the joy and peace I receive from You become a testament to Your faithfulness for others to witness and believe. Amen.

10

REMEMBERING HE IS FAITHFUL

While it's true that you can't move forward in life by looking in the rear-view mirror, sometimes you can move forward in your faith by looking back at the ways God has been faithful on the winding road that got you to the present.

Imagine David in a very tight spot as he awaited word on Absalom's murderous intentions, "These things I remember as I pour out my soul: how I used to go to the house of God under the protection of the Mighty One with shouts of joy and praise among the festive throng" (Psalm 42:4). His mind was likely wandering back to his days of leading worship in Jerusalem.

In the same way, when we focus on the things God has done for us in the past, that helps us to overcome difficulty. For instance, one of the best things you can do when you have a family argument is to get out the photo album. Look at pictures that bring back memories of God's blessings. It's amazing how the simple act of looking back can change the atmosphere, and how restoration is allowed to flow as we recall blessed times together.

Try this with a current area of strife. What is your deepest need? What do you cry out to God about in this season of your life? Consider how God has responded to your prayers and pleading in the past. Spend time looking through a mental photo album of the time when you heard, felt, or saw God's hand in your circumstance. Will He not do the same for you now?

God reminded His people again and again of His redeeming act of delivering them from slavery. Many of the psalms focus on God as Deliverer and recall instances where He saved His people from calamity. In Psalms 105, 106, and 107 we read lengthy offerings celebrating the Israelites' deliverance. Reciting these psalms reminded the people of what God had already done for them and therefore what He would do for them again.

David looked forward to seeing God do a similar work of deliverance in his own life.

As the king of Israel remembers God's goodness, he lets the Holy Spirit challenge his lagging soul. David revisited God's faithfulness and used chosen memories as a bridge to the future. He cheered himself up by looking back, but then he moved forward. Moving forward is the necessary next step.

I can imagine David's thought process: *All of my past experience shows me that God has not withdrawn from me nor abandoned me. So what makes me think He would abandon me now? I will put my hope in God, and I will praise Him once again.* The remedy for David's despair was to turn to God, to thirst after God, and to put his hope in God.

When your hurt or need transforms into a thirst for God to show His faithfulness, you will see evidence of His response to your cries. This time in your history will become a part of your testimony. A snapshot of God's tenderness toward your pain today will become one to return to for encouragement when you face difficulties again.

If dark clouds are covering your life, get ready! God is about to part the clouds and shower you with blessings. If you have learned to find your contentment in obedience to God, and if you trust that God will shine His light into your darkness, then He will bring peace and restoration to your situation.

People use the adage "This too shall pass" for good reason when talking with someone facing a troubled time. As believers, we can *know* this with certainty because we know the clouds of adversity will pass over us eventually. God doesn't always remove the reason we are suffering, but He is always there to dispel the darkness and be our guiding light through it. Don't ever forget that.

For you, LORD, have delivered me from death,
> my eyes from tears,
> my feet from stumbling,
that I may walk before the LORD
> in the land of the living.

PSALM 116:8-9

Dear God, in times when I feel alone or abandoned, I will remember Your faithfulness. The worries plaguing my mind and filling my prayers today are reasons to praise You because later they will be a part of stories of Your provision and deliverance. With gratitude I look back on times when You have saved me from myself or from the detours I have taken down unhealthy paths. What a blessing that You do not keep a tally of my sins, Lord. Instead, You forget them and forgive me.

Covered in grace, I have hope that the clouds will pass as I meditate on all You have done and await the light that is to come. In Your mercy You do not abandon me. Instead, You lovingly shepherd me into the land of the living. I will spend my days recalling and telling of Your goodness. Amen.

PURPOSE IN OBEDIENCE

Just as sin and rebellion can create restlessness in our hearts, the opposite can also be true. Sometimes God wants to see if we will follow Him in obedience even when we're not aware of the purpose behind it. He may call us out of our comfort zones and into unfamiliar realms that initially make us restless.

Have you felt the discomfort of obedience? The easy path is rarely the one God requires us to walk to show our willingness to shed our own agenda and plans. In fact, when He calls you forward to be obedient to His purpose, you may start out on a journey that feels a bit like going uphill in the wilderness. While you are searching for familiar landmarks and signs, God is asking you to forget the map and trust His leading instead.

David was driven from Jerusalem by the murderous plotting of his son, and Joseph, another hero of the Old Testament, became an exile not by volunteering for the job, but because it was part of God's plan. Joseph's wandering was forced upon him when his brothers sold him into slavery. But unlike his great-grandfather Abraham, Joseph left his home without the benefit of God's promise that his sojourning was part of a bigger divine scheme.

It's difficult for us to accept that obedience to God would lead to slavery, false accusations, and imprisonment. Yet all of those happened to Joseph, who remained uncomplaining in his obedience to God. When we read his story, we learn that Joseph was yanked from his home to become an exile in Egypt because God needed him there.

When Joseph was a teenager, he had dreams of playing a prominent role both in his family and among his people. These dreams stirred a growing awareness that someday he would be used by God. Because Joseph was never secretive about his dreams, his brothers conspired to kill him. Instead of killing him, however, they sold him into slavery (see Genesis 37:12-36).

If we were formulating the path to greatness, none of us would ever include these steps: 1) become a slave, 2) get thrown into prison on false charges, and 3) hope that somehow we would be released. But Joseph endured these injustices year after year. And when the time was right, God elevated him to a position of astounding prominence. Joseph became prime minister of Egypt, second in power only to the pharaoh (see Genesis 43:1-34).

In retrospect Joseph could see that it was God who had sent him to Egypt. When his family came to Egypt to buy food, Joseph told them, "Do not be distressed and do not be angry with yourselves for selling me here, because it was to save lives that God sent me ahead of you…You intended to harm me, but God intended it for good" (Genesis 45:5; 50:20).

In a movie with a similar story arc, this would be the moment the hero would reinforce his innocence, enforce his power, and force his oppressors into a dreadful fate. But Joseph saw beyond his human trials. He understood that his obedience and suffering were exactly what led to eventual greatness and the preservation of his family—the family that eventually grew to become the nation of Israel.

Maybe you are in a place or circumstance that feels counterintuitive to your understanding of what life should look like at this juncture, age, or part of your faith story. But God's view is so much more expansive than yours. He knows the people you will eventually meet and influence. He celebrates the victories you have no idea are ahead. He sees the impact your lived-out faith will have on generations to come. If you look around and think, *Is this it? Is this the life of faithfulness?*, keep watching and trusting. God has a purpose and an intention for good that will unfold because of your obedience.

I seek you with all my heart;
    do not let me stray from your commands.
I have hidden your word in my heart
    that I might not sin against you.

PSALM 119:10-11

Lord, it's my desire to be obedient to You, for I know You have a unique plan for my life. I can't see up ahead, but You can. You know what today's faithfulness will bring about tomorrow. What a privilege it is to know my life will be used for Your purposes, Lord. My obedience is my offering, and to You it is better than a sacrifice.

When I am about to falter, I will trust that these times of wandering or uncertainty are not wasted. As I move in the direction of Your will and Your way, You are using my words, actions, and times of waiting for Your good and Your glory. I will seek You with all my heart. Even when I am uncomfortable or must face the darkness, do not let me stray from Your commands. There is too much at stake. Amen.

12

WHEN RESTLESSNESS
IS REDEEMED

Few would equate a season of restlessness with progress. Few would welcome the angst and discomfort of uncertainty with a vague hope that *maybe* such a season will eventually lead to contentment. When we are unsure of what is to come or where we are going, that space for doubt or anxiousness grows. But our concern grows from the soil of our human perspective rather than God's view and plan. The One who can take what we might discard and make it beautiful, powerful, and meaningful is, thankfully, the One we were made to trust and follow…even into a time of restlessness.

It's important to realize that the restlessness that God stirred in many of the biblical heroes' lives led not only to the redemption of the individual involved, but also extended to bless untold future generations. In obedience to God, Abraham left his livelihood and his home to become a homeless wanderer. It was through the wandering of Abraham that God set into motion His plan of redemption for humankind.

When he left Mesopotamia, Abram had no destination. God simply told him, "Go from your country, your people and your father's household and go to the land I will show you" (Genesis 12:1). The Lord also promised that He would make a great nation out of Abram's descendants, and He changed his name from Abram, meaning "exalted father," to Abraham, "father of many nations" (see Genesis 17:5).

Can you imagine encountering a God who is foreign to your own culture, hearing Him tell you to leave for an undisclosed location, and then doing it? And once you obey that initial command, God changes your name and tells you He will make a mighty nation out of you? You want to believe this part, but you're an old man, and your elderly wife has always been infertile.

Most of us would start questioning our sanity at that point. And, certainly, others around us would whisper about our failed sense of reason. But Abraham continued to follow God. His sojourn eventually brought him to a city that was destined to be dedicated to the worship of God, a city where people of all nationalities and backgrounds would come in the distant future to learn about the true God.

Abraham first encountered this city when he paid tribute to Melchizedek, the priest-king of Salem, which means "peace." Both the Psalms and the New Testament tell us that Melchizedek, whose name means "king of righteousness," was a type of Christ, our Prince of Peace and King of Righteousness. It would be almost a thousand years after Abraham first entered Salem that King David would conquer the city from the Jebusites, and Jerusalem would finally become the center for worship of almighty God.

God had in mind a city where He would be honored and worshipped, a place where people could congregate to learn about Him. With Abraham, and later with David, God made provision for that city. Jerusalem would become known as the City of God. But as glorious as this city was, it was only God's temporary provision, a mere foreshadowing of the Eternal City of God that is still to come.

God knows the long game and invites us to play our part at different junctures. Abraham faithfully entered a time of restlessness because he chose to follow God. In his lifetime he saw some promises of God fulfilled; however, he did not see all that was to come or understand all the reasons God asked him to walk forward in faith.

If God has been calling you to walk forward, act boldly, or stretch in a new direction that requires you to bear the discomfort of restlessness, be encouraged. Your yes to God will not be wasted. It will be used to glorify His name in your life. It will be used to further His plan and bring others to the Eternal City of God.

———

Although the Lord gives you the bread of adversity and the water of affliction, your teachers will be hidden no more; with your own eyes you will see them. Whether you turn to the right or to the left, your ears will hear a voice behind you, saying, "This is the way; walk in it."

ISAIAH 30:20-21

Heavenly Father, give me the faith of Your servant Abraham, who answered Your call without hesitation. He faced what would look to the world as a journey of risk, loss, and possible futility, and yet he still said yes. In my daily life, I am used to having a map before I enter unknown terrain. Sometimes, to say yes to what You ask me to do, I must face the restlessness and discomfort of full surrender with incomplete information.

My part in Your long game is not for me to understand. I may not have a map or insight into Your plan, but I do have faith in You. You ask me to trust and not be afraid. Guide me today by Your loving voice and reveal Your will to me. When I hear You say, "This is the way; walk in it," I am ready with my yes. Amen.

$$\left(\begin{array}{c}13\end{array}\right)$$

THE GLORY OF THE LORD

When our discontent springs from a burning hunger for God, we will be compelled to seek Him with our whole hearts, and He will allow us to find Him.

Some believers hold back from seeking God because they carry guilt from their sinful actions or lackluster faith. However, the good news is that if your deepest desire is to bring glory to God, then He will overcome the weakness in your life just as He did with David.

When we know we can turn to God yet again for help and not be turned away, our hearts expand with gratitude and a desire to honor the Lord. And when we desire to honor the Lord Jesus Christ, God will pour out a blessing on us. So in a way that only our loving God could construct, our times of struggle actually lead us to the mercy of His blessings.

God looked beyond mankind's rebellion and permitted the flawed David to set aside a city that would bring glory to God. In spite of—or perhaps because of—his sin, David had a deep desire to revere God. When he repented, David longed to be in God's presence. And God blessed him. In a sovereign act of grace and election, the Lord honored David's desire to build Jerusalem into a center of worship.

In turn, David expressed his love, devotion, and praise through the many psalms he authored. When you read his writings, it's obvious just how deeply he delighted in God's presence. The temple musicians used many of David's psalms for public worship, and today the church still sings these psalms. Later, when Solomon dedicated the temple in Jerusalem, the temple his father had dreamed of building, God's glory fell upon the worshippers. "When Solomon finished praying, fire came down from heaven and consumed the burnt offering and the sacrifices, and the glory of the LORD filled the temple. The priests could not enter the temple of the LORD because the glory of the LORD filled it" (2 Chronicles 7:1-2).

Wherever God is sought, He will show up in all His glory.

Earthly Jerusalem and its temple were only a dim representation of what it means for God to indwell the praises of His people. They were a rough sketch of what can happen when the glory of God is fully revealed. In this life we can't fully comprehend what it means for God to be with us all the time. Why? Because on Earth, our discontent often leads us to run away from Him. We tend to forget His commandments and close our ears to His voice. Instead, we are seduced by the voices and the standards of the world system. In the heavenly Jerusalem, however, we will have unending communion with God. There will be no one to whisper doubts, fear, or anxiety in our ears. We will be fully restored to communion with Him.

In the meantime, as we look ahead to the New Jerusalem, we can have intimacy with the God who longs to fellowship with us. When our inner discontent stirs, we can look at our lives and consider the state of our hearts. Are we experiencing God's glory by desiring to glorify Him, or are we fumbling along, complaining and asking for help now and then in moments of frustration yet unwilling to tend to the state of our spirits? If our search for communion with God comes only through petitions for our desires to be fulfilled, we won't experience the amazing light and glory of the Lord.

Let us be like David and express our love and devotion to God. Praise His name. Cry out with gratitude no matter your circumstances. Sing of His mercy and grace. We don't want to miss out on the full presence of God and the blessings that come from the pure, wholehearted pursuit of Him.

⁓

Create in me a pure heart, O God,
 and renew a steadfast spirit within me.
Do not cast me from your presence
 or take your Holy Spirit from me.

PSALM 51:10-11

Lord, I want to live a life that is honoring to You so that I may enjoy the blessing of uninterrupted fellowship with You. Like David, I want to seek You always, including the times when I am at my lowest. Even when I hide my fear from others, I trust that my weaknesses will be overcome by Your strength. When I am afraid or anxious, You instill in me a steadfast spirit and a hope that carries me through.

God, I'm grateful You don't cast me away but choose to use my life for Your purpose. Give me a pure heart that is filled with Your light and knowledge. I love You and long for the day when I will experience perfect contentment in Your presence. Show me today how I can draw closer to You and bring You glory in my daily life. Amen.

14

RETURNING TO THE FATHER

It's likely we are all familiar with the song "Amazing Grace." If we had to have one song to hum every day or name as our soundtrack, I think this should be it. Why? Because the action of grace should constantly spark our awe. There is perhaps no more powerful depiction of God's amazing grace than the story of the prodigal son. In this story we witness the repentant return of a wayward son into the arms of a grace-filled father. God's welcoming grace is the place where discontent begins to fade.

Unlike Abraham and Joseph, whose sojourns began in obedience to either God's call or His intervention, the prodigal son left home out of willfulness. He insisted on getting what was his, turning his back on his father. In his certainty that life was far better out in the world, he gave little thought to the riches of provision and family he was leaving behind. The loving father could only watch his son's figure disappear into the distance.

But the son eventually reached a turning point, and the story has a joyous ending. Unlike Cain and Nimrod, who refused to repent and turn back to God, the prodigal son ended his sinful wandering when he reached the end of himself. He had strayed so far, and now he was hungry, dirty, and tired as he took work to feed someone's pigs. He realized that even the pigs were eating better than he was. It was then that he recalled his father's love and care and longed to return to him. "'I will set out and go back to my father and say to him: Father, I have sinned against heaven and against you. I am no longer worthy to be called your son; make me like one of your hired servants.' So he got up and went to his father" (Luke 15:18-20).

He returned home as a broken, repentant son. He wasn't sure what his homecoming would be like or if he would be received, but in his heart, he was trusting the love of his father that he knew from his early life.

If you have trouble relating to the accomplishments of biblical heroes and heroines, then think of your life in light of the prodigal son. He was an ordinary person who showed no great courage and was never a great leader, but he did remember his father when his wandering fed him the bitter fruit that comes from disobedience. Most of us can identify with the prodigal son who brought despair and humiliation upon himself.

Like this young man, we may find ourselves wandering far from the Father who loves us. Often, we recognize that we're putting distance between ourselves and God, but still we continue on our way. You may not have run from family or responsibilities, but maybe your mind and heart are turned away from God. The space between you and the Father's will is growing daily because you don't look to His Word or return to Him in prayer when you've wandered.

Take stock of where you are in your version of the story of the prodigal. Are you yet at the end of yourself and tired of being exhausted by the world and the pursuits of what it claims to offer? Are you weary and longing to be back in the care of the Father who knew you before you were born and is eager to have you home in His presence? If you can confess your sin and mistakes and surrender your pride to circle back to your home in God, you are ready for the rest of the story to unfold in your own life.

The glorious news in Scripture is that while we experiment with life apart from God, He patiently waits for us to return. And He welcomes us home with the joy and warm embrace that we see in this grace-filled story.

While he was still a long way off, his father saw him and was filled with compassion for him; he ran to his son, threw his arms around him and kissed him.

LUKE 15:20

Father, there are times You have watched me walk away from Your will, purpose, or principles. I've been cold in my pursuit of You or distant in my worship. I become distracted by work and worries. Envy pulls my gaze off You and onto what I think my life should be...and that makes me want to run from what is and do things in my own power.

Seek Your servant, Lord, for I have not forgotten Your commands. I place my trust in You because You have made me alive in Christ even when I was dead in my transgressions. By Your grace You have promised to save me. My heart softens and my will opens to You when I realize You stand as forgiving Father, not as judge, as You welcome me back to Your love, the life You have for me, and that amazing grace. Amen.

15

GIFTED WITH GRACE

The free gift of God's grace goes against every human instinct and every other religious system. The Buddhist eightfold path, the Hindu doctrine of karma, the Jewish ceremonial law, and the Islamic shari'ah law all require followers to earn divine approval. Only Jesus Christ, through whom the world was created, offers unconditional love. Only God in human flesh could be so extravagant in His generosity.

But why would God continue to offer us His gift of grace, especially after we rebel and wander far from Him? God's nature won't allow Him to do anything other than to pursue those who are lost. Most in our society are more interested in exercising their rights than their righteousness made possible through God's grace. Most people believe they can be good on their own without relying on God. While many would love to have God bless them with abundance, achievement, and healthy families, they live their lives as though it's their positive thinking, determination, and sweat equity that make things happen. This is a very self-focused and terribly exhausting way to be.

Plenty of believers worship and pray on Sunday, and then when Monday comes, their nose is to the grindstone—or to their personal devices—to shape their fate and success as though God has nothing to do with real life. (Even though God is the Author of real life!)

Many others fall somewhere in the middle. They are aware of the continuing search for a better life, for peace and fulfillment, but they fail to see that the only hope for their restoration is God and His grace. They still carry the burden to carve out the direction of their lives as well as seek the glory when good things unfold. But this is not a life surrendered to the gift of grace.

Scripture describes two types of grace. The first is what theologians refer to as "common grace," but more accurately it should be called "mercy," which is freely given to everyone. God "causes his sun to rise on the evil and the good and sends rain on the righteous and the unrighteous" (Matthew 5:45). The beauty of God's creation is free for everyone to enjoy, whether they follow God or not. Nonbelievers are not blind to a glorious sunrise, nor are they blocked from receiving compassion from hearts moved by God's goodness.

In contrast to God's mercy, however, His grace is given exclusively to those who belong to Christ. This grace is lavished only upon those who have accepted the sacrifice of God's Son and received Him as their Savior and Lord. This grace is the unmerited, inexhaustible, and irresistible favor of God. This is the grace that restores us—satisfying our longing for contentment. To constantly revel in the God of grace and the grace of God is the most exhilarating aspect of the Christian life.

Which kind of grace have you experienced for most of your days? I hope it is the latter, my friend. If so, you know what it feels like to lean into God's presence with complete assurance that He is there…in that real life you are living. You know the relief of forgiveness and the power of it to flood you with gratitude for your Lord. And you know the confidence that comes from being guided by God along the journey.

If you have been blessed by mercy but not changed by grace, let today be your invitation to accept the gift of your Savior. There are no limits to what His grace can and will do in your life. The discontent or disconnection you have sensed will be transformed into contentment and connection in Christ.

Today, walk with the lightness, purpose, and joy of being a child of God who has accepted the unconditional love and grace of Jesus. Live, give, serve, and worship with a freedom the world longs for.

It is by grace you have been saved, through faith—and this is not from yourselves, it is the gift of God—not by works, so that no one can boast.

EPHESIANS 2:8-9

Lord, I don't take for granted the gift of Your grace—the reason I have been saved. The grace that covers me and lifts me up cannot be earned by works, yet it is Your grace that allows me to abound in good works and serve You and others.

When I begin to feel restless, I will stop and consider the undeserved favor You have bestowed upon me. You know Your servant is flawed, but again and again You receive me, bless me, forgive me, and protect me. In Your mercy, You take me into Your presence and hear all that I lift up to You. Thank You for listening to me and for extending Your grace. All that I have comes from You—my shelter, friends, provision, the work of my days, and every blessing I've known. I praise You for Your unending goodness. Amen.

16

REMEDY FOR OUR THORNS

As we set our feet on a new path, we need to be aware of attitudes, habits, and circumstances that can cause us to veer off course. If we're not aware of these detours, we'll lose the peace and contentment of God. The first detour we need to recognize is that of personal weaknesses.

We all go through times when we're trying to move ahead in life, but just as we pull into the passing lane to get around an 18-wheeler, another truck comes roaring down the highway from the opposite direction. We're merely trying to make progress, but we're staring imminent danger right in the eyes—or right in the headlights, as the case may be.

At some point, life beats us down. It might be the loss of a loved one, a doctor's terrifying diagnosis, or the betrayal of a friend. Whenever these types of situations threaten to overcome us, we can either rely on our own resources or we can admit our helplessness and draw on the outpouring of God's grace.

We most readily recognize our need for God when we are the weakest. The weaker we become, the more we pray. And the more we pray, the more God's strength is made perfect in our weakness. The apostle Paul faced the threatening rush of human weakness and begged God to remove the source. Paul had been given a "thorn in the flesh," a constant reminder of his human frailty. Whatever Paul's thorn was, we know it was no minor irritation.

It's no accident that the Holy Spirit, who authored the Scriptures, did not specify what Paul's problem was. By not knowing the exact nature of his suffering, we can all imagine Paul hurting with whatever hurts us. And as we limp along in our human frailty, we can identify with Paul's initial longing for God to remove the thorn.

As you confront the thorns in your life, it's important to recognize their potential to pull you away from contentment. Even when you pursue the peace that comes from God's grace, you can be derailed by painful circumstances. To avoid detours, keep in mind these truths.

Satan is the manufacturer of thorns. Paul described his thorn as "a messenger of Satan" that had been sent to torment him (2 Corinthians 12:7). Satan never sends you love messages. His messages will always put dread in your heart. Identifying Satan as the source helps us put our thorns in perspective.

God's grace takes away the sting. Don't allow Satan's torments to make you doubt that God will bring good out of bad. Don't permit Satan to convince you that God doesn't love you enough to give you grace for every moment. Whatever thorns are causing you to suffer, God is using them for your own protection. You may be weary of the thorns, but be assured that God can take away the sting.

God's grace brings roses out of thorns. Paul did not ask for grace, but God gave him grace anyway. Grace is the spiritual power to live triumphantly no matter what our circumstances are. Grace also provides the spiritual ability to see the rose that is about to blossom amid the briar patch.

Grace always shines the brightest against the darkness of our circumstances. If God's grace is not sufficient for you, then it may be that you are focusing so much on the thorn that you can't see the rose of God's grace developing in you. Once our concerns are left at the feet of our Lord, we can trust that His grace is entirely sufficient. It's the only balm to remove Satan's sting of dread and doubt. Apart from it, there is no peace, no rest, and no contentment.

Give over your troubles to the Lord and surrender your weaknesses. His grace is the remedy for your thorns and the redemption for your pain.

He has said to me, "My grace is sufficient for you, for power is perfected in weakness." Most gladly, therefore, I will rather boast about my weaknesses, so that the power of Christ may dwell in me.

2 Corinthians 12:9 (lsb)

Father, it's difficult to confront my weaknesses. Human pride tempts me to deny my flaws. But in light of Your promise to be my strength, I confess my shortcomings. Help me to place my confidence only in You so that I may receive, as Paul did, the comfort of Your grace. My personal thorns are a gift because they humble me, turn me to You for help, and show others that my accomplishments and triumphs are only possible through Your power and not my own.

God, I know that You are not the author of the pain and trials that torment me. Instead, these things are fiery darts from the Enemy. When I become discouraged, help me remember that Your grace is completely sufficient for all of my needs. My fear is natural for a human, but my salvation and hope are supernatural in You and the remedy of Your grace. Amen.

17

BY THE GRACE OF GOD

When we are given the gift to live under God's grace, our life is infused with His love, joy, and beauty. Our hope is bright, and our communion with the Lord is deep and meaningful. But something brews within religious communities that can undermine our relationship with the Lord if we aren't careful. It's called legalism.

Sadly, those who get caught in the trap of legalism likely started the journey to God's heart with the pure desire to find contentment and His acceptance. But when a person's faith becomes more about abiding by man-made rules and less about God's mercy and commands, the truth is twisted into a lie that says salvation comes through God's grace *plus* our effort.

Friend, don't ever believe this lie. I grew up in legalism and have experienced firsthand its power to steal our joy in living and walking daily in the presence of Christ.

Paul wrote his letter to the Christians in Galatia to combat the false doctrine of legalism—the faulty notion that God's grace is merely a beginning and that continuing the journey of the Christian life requires our striving and earning. The falsehood might look like believing a certain religious dogma, practicing a ritual or sacrament, performing specific good deeds, or avoiding certain peculiarities of outward appearance, such as requiring that women wear a head covering.

The "shoulds" created by men are not the same as God's commands. We are saved by God's grace alone, through faith alone, and even that faith is not our own; it's God's gift to us.

Legalists often tell their followers that if they fail to adhere to certain man-made requirements and prohibitions, they are in danger of losing their salvation. This is often referred to as "falling from grace." But such use of this phrase creates confusion.

Don't fall for the falsehood that a Christian can forfeit his or her salvation. It runs contrary to the words of Jesus: "All those the Father gives me will come to me, and whoever comes to me I will never drive away...And this is the will of him who sent me, that I shall lose none of all those he has given me, but raise them up at the last day" (John 6:37, 39).

It's tragic that many Christians lack joy, peace, and hope simply because they don't know if they will go to heaven. But God tells us that we can be sure of our salvation. God finishes what He starts, and His grace is "able to keep you from stumbling and to present you before his glorious presence without fault and with great joy" (Jude 24).

In his letter to the Galatians, Paul wrote: "You who are trying to be justified by the law have been alienated from Christ; you have fallen away from grace" (Galatians 5:4). He did not use the expression "fallen from grace" to mean that a Christian could lose his or her salvation, but what did he mean? It's clear from the context that he was talking about legalism.

To sin and then to repent and ask for God's grace in forgiveness is not falling from grace. But relying on your own ability to adhere to certain rules and rituals as the basis of your righteousness is clearly stumbling away from God's grace. Choosing legalism is abandoning grace as the basis of your relationship with God. Release your trust in your own efforts. Place your trust only in the all-sufficient work of Christ in salvation.

Friend, don't abandon the grace that comes freely to you as a believer. Allow yourself to be immersed in that grace and its assurance. When legalistic ideas come your way, you will know they don't represent the love of the Lord. Your footing is secure in your salvation, and by God's grace—not your effort—that will not change.

———

You also were included in Christ when you heard the message of truth, the gospel of your salvation. When you believed, you were marked in him with a seal, the promised Holy Spirit, who is a deposit guaranteeing our inheritance until the redemption of those who are God's possession—to the praise of his glory.

EPHESIANS 1:13-14

Lord, thank You that Your grace alone is sufficient to save me. The man-made requirements of legalism don't breathe new life into me. Instead, they limit my hope and what I can accomplish in You. The trap of legalism keeps my attention on man's rules instead of on Your commands and mercy. I want to be immersed in the joy of a relationship with You. As I am obedient to Your will, I will gladly make sacrifices because they are not made for human approval but are instead made to glorify You.

A life spent in fear and shame is not the grace-filled life Your redemption provides. Despite my inherited sin nature, my eternal future is secure because of the sacrifice made on the cross by Jesus Christ. By Your grace I am forever saved and in the embrace of Your unconditional love. Amen.

18

TRADE PRIDE FOR PRAYER

Sometimes we experience the good restlessness of being nudged out of our comfort zones by God to be obedient and faithful. However, there is another kind of restlessness that brews in us when we think we deserve better than our current situation and decide to find contentment on our own. This usually sparks us to follow our sinful nature and a path of pride.

Pride is a powerful force, and it's also deceptive. We can talk ourselves into believing that our choices are motivated by a desire to do good when, in fact, we are motivated by a hunger to do what's best for ourselves. Setting aside our own agenda starts with accepting God's invitation to come boldly before His throne of grace in prayer. With such an invitation extended to us, how can we possibly neglect the pursuit of prayer? Part of the problem is that life can become too comfortable.

Ask the typical Christian how long he or she spends in personal prayer time when everything is going well, and you'll probably be met with a good deal of hemming and hawing. So many of us are crisis prayer warriors. The Enemy of our soul knows that prayer is the source of our strength. Therefore he does all that is within his power to cut our supply lines and undermine our habit of prayer.

And aside from the Enemy's distraction tactics, perhaps the biggest enemy of prayer is pride. Pride tells us that everything we need can be achieved through human effort if we just invest enough time and enough energy. That sounds logical, but it's a lie. It's no wonder we get into such desperate spiritual trouble when we neglect prayer.

Many of us neglect our prayer lives because we don't comprehend the awesome privilege of praying. We simply do not understand God's eagerness to answer our prayers. And we fail to appreciate the power of connectedness with the Almighty that comes through our seeking communication with Him.

In a time of crisis, Queen Esther approached the king's throne in fear. It was against the law to come before the king without his invitation. Had the king not extended the royal scepter, signifying his willingness to grant her an audience, Esther could have been put to death. But the king was pleased to see her, even though she appeared unannounced and uninvited.

If a human king could extend grace to an uninvited visitor, how much more is God willing to extend grace to us when we approach Him in prayer? After all, we already have an invitation to come before God's throne and to beseech Him for whatever we need.

Here is the amazing invitation God has extended to us:

> Since we have a great high priest who has ascended into heaven, Jesus the Son of God, let us hold firmly to the faith we profess. For we do not have a high priest who is unable to empathize with our weaknesses, but we have one who has been tempted in every way, just as we are—yet he did not sin. Let us then approach God's throne of grace with confidence, so that we may receive mercy and find grace to help us in our time of need (Hebrews 4:14-16).

We need not approach God in fear, worrying whether He will receive us. When we have accepted Christ as our Savior, we are invited to enter the royal throne room. We have a right to be there, and it's our privilege to pour out our hearts to God. All who are followers of the Lord Jesus Christ are invited to experience the awesomeness of the power of the grace of God in prayer.

The Spirit helps us in our weakness. We do not know what we ought to pray for, but the Spirit himself intercedes for us through wordless groans. And he who searches our hearts knows the mind of the Spirit, because the Spirit intercedes for God's people in accordance with the will of God.

Romans 8:26-27

Lord, at times I have fallen for the Enemy's distractions and not called out to You in prayer because of my pride. Other times I have not prayed because I didn't know how to express my feelings to You. There have been days when I have felt unworthy to come to You because of guilt or because my problems seem embarrassingly small compared to the massive needs of the world. But Your Word tells me that I can approach You and Your throne with confidence. I know that if I ask anything according to Your will, You will hear me.

Today I stand before You and claim Your promise that Your Holy Spirit will make sense of the unspoken and spoken expressions of my spirit. What an amazing privilege it is to pray knowing You receive me as Your child because of my faith in Your Son, Jesus. Amen.

19

LONGING FOR HEAVEN

In our first devotions, we looked at how the loss of contentment steals peace from our hearts and leads to destructive attempts to quiet our restlessness and longings. We have also seen that true peace comes only through God's grace. The highest experience of peace and contentment is found in a life of obedience to God.

Still, earthly peace and contentment are but shadows of what is to come. A day looms in the future when God will judge the world so He can establish the heavenly Jerusalem, where His children will enjoy the Lord's presence forever.

The longing in our spirit for this future home and our eternity in God's presence can arise and leave us bothered by the state of things in the world and in our circumstances. We may feel as though we can't get to heaven fast enough. We bear burdens. Our human bodies experience pain or weakness and eventually grow old. We witness loved ones hurting or dying. We feel the weight of decisions. We are frustrated by our failings even when we live under God's grace.

At a certain point we understand that as we maneuver life on Earth and long for heaven, we are a part of the story of the children of God, the people we've had glimpses of in this devotional so far and those we have studied more in depth in church or on our own.

God began human history in a paradise known as the Garden of Eden, where the first humans enjoyed unhindered fellowship with God. Likewise, God will close earthly history with a garden city, a heavenly city known as the New Jerusalem. In that city, we will dwell with Him for eternity. And that, at long last, will put an end to our longing for more.

In the book of Revelation, we read about the permanent dwelling place for everyone who has placed their faith in Christ. In this promised garden city, we will be fully restored to the intimate communion with God for which we were created. At long last our wandering will end.

When Adam and Eve were evicted from the Garden of Eden, humanity began looking for a city. Cain and his descendants foolishly sought a home in the rebellious city of man. But God promises a heavenly city, the place that Abraham looked forward to, "the city with foundations, whose architect and builder is God" (Hebrews 11:10). This city of God has foundations, which implies permanence, and for that reason we often refer to it as the Eternal City.

The ancient city of Jerusalem foreshadowed "the city that is to come" (Hebrews 13:14). The Bible also refers to this future city as "the heavenly Jerusalem" (Hebrews 12:22) and "the Holy City, the new Jerusalem" (Revelation 21:2). Earthly Jerusalem was considered a holy city because God allowed Solomon to build a "home" for Him there. From that time forward, the temple became the focal point for worshipping God in the Hebrew faith. But as Christians, we have now become the temples of the Holy Spirit (see 1 Corinthians 6:19). There is no longer a need for an earthly temple because the ultimate sacrifice for sin has been offered once and for all in Jesus.

Sometimes we struggle so much to keep the proper perspective between the earthly realm and the eternal that we lose an awareness of our heavenly future. Heaven is not just a far-off vacation spot we'll visit someday. As believers in Christ, we are already citizens of heaven—and when you look at it that way, life on planet Earth is nothing more than a short layover before we enter our heavenly home.

The day will come when you will be in God's presence in a way that exceeds our human imagination. Until then, allow your longings to lead you again and again to His heart and His will.

Do you not know that your bodies are temples of the Holy Spirit, who is in you, whom you have received from God? You are not your own; you were bought at a price.

1 Corinthians 6:19-20

What a blessing it is, Lord, to rest assured in the knowledge that You give eternal life. No one can snatch me from Your hand. Help me see my earthly life in the proper perspective as I look forward to the ultimate place of peace—my heavenly home. Don't let me confuse my longing for an eternity with You for any earthly wants.

You have placed the Holy Spirit in me, and I trust His leading. When I ache for something other than You, may the Spirit remind me of the desires You have placed on my heart. On this journey I don't want to miss out on the goodness You have for me. There are blessings of heaven to savor in this human, earthly life: wisdom, truth, love, compassion, service, peace, forgiveness, grace, and more. I'm grateful, Lord, because this is just a taste of what is to come. Amen.

$$\binom{20}{}$$

CONTENTMENT IN GOD

The Bible tells us that our heavenly home offers beauty beyond comprehension along with a permanent end to our restlessness. Why, then, are Christians apt to forget that ultimate contentment comes from God and that we will never fully experience rest and peace until we enter heaven? Have you struggled along in a particular pursuit, thinking you were doing something true and right for your life, only to wake up one day and realize your goal was far from God's best for you? Temporary contentment eventually gave way to an eternal truth that things of the world will never satisfy.

Here are few reasons I believe we confuse earthly gains for spiritual contentment.

False perceptions. Most of us fail to dwell on the magnificent glory of heaven, and because that ultimate objective is distant from our thoughts and priorities, we settle for the world's distractions that look right and true when they are shiny, appealing, and temporarily satisfy us. We don't recognize their lies because we aren't holding up God's vision, truth, and hope as our pursuit.

Life's pressures. The emotional wear and tear of life can steal our attention away from eternal matters. But the Lord wants us to be faithful even while we face demanding responsibilities. He wants us to serve Him in all we do so that we can draw the attention of the world to the Savior. We must let people know that we live the way we do because we have a home in heaven and that they, too, may be forgiven and enjoy eternity in the New Jerusalem.

The allure of what is seen. Whatever we see receives our immediate attention. Heaven is "out of sight," therefore it often remains "out of mind." We tend to believe what is verifiable, and we usually prefer to verify things visually. Then we fall into the trap of believing that the life we can see will go on forever, so we invest everything we have in this life while neglecting the spiritual life.

The church's worldliness. The early church measured success in terms of eternal gain, not membership growth or financial prosperity. Today many people preach health and wealth here on Earth. Why would anyone spend time thinking about heaven if they believe they can get everything they want right here? If we feast on the world's banquet, our spirit's hunger for eternity increases *and* remains unmet. The bigger house or more coveted job will not ease the unrest—earthly gains may fuel unrest more if we're not looking through an eternal lens.

False doctrine. The majority of Americans think they will automatically go to heaven when they die. And, amazingly, many churches are teaching that God saves everyone. The truth is that there is a literal hell, but those who end up there are not sent there by God. Those who enter hell send themselves there by refusing God's provision for their salvation.

God woos us, longing to hold us in His embrace. Our lack of satisfaction in life, our restlessness, our loss of peace—all of these should bring us to the end of ourselves, where we will finally turn and seek God's grace.

Our home, our place of rest and contentment, is with God. If you have left God's presence to wander the desert of self or to create a life apart from Him, may you feel the pull to restore fellowship with the Father. If you have stayed in close relationship with God, may you now see how the times of discontent, need, and restlessness point you back to a longing for deeper intimacy with God and His will for you. Consider how God's grace meets you in any current discontent. How is the balm of His love transforming you?

Let us live with the comfort and assurance of God as our refuge and strength—our hope that is immediate, transformative, personal, and eternal.

Godliness with contentment is great gain. For we brought nothing into the world, and we can take nothing out of it.

1 Timothy 6:6-7

Lord, so many distractions are in the world. Please help me focus less on that which is temporal and more on what is everlasting. My agitation and impatience lead me to grasp in desperation at short-term fixes. Instead, I want to fix my eyes on heaven and Your enduring love. Free me from false perceptions and teachings. Give me an ear that knows the sound of Your truth immediately and a heart that wants that truth.

Instill in me, Father, the patience to grow in my faith as I wait for what You have for me. As I come to You in earnest prayer, there is a calm that pervades my body and spirit. My discontent turns to contentment, and restlessness turns to peace. I am released from the desire to acquire the world's trappings. You provide all I need to live a godly, contented life following You. Amen.

FINDING HEALING
IN HIS HOPE

I lift up my eyes to the mountains—
where does my help come from?
*My help comes from the L*ord*,*
the Maker of heaven and earth.

Psalm 121:1-2

He heals the brokenhearted
and binds up their wounds.

PSALM 147:3

Intuitively, we all sense that we are not whole physically, emotionally, or spiritually. And we possess within us a deep need to be made whole. Given the fundamental nature of this human need, it is not surprising that healing and spirituality have become intertwined in the modern world.

Time after time, men and women suffering from life-threatening illnesses are told by the best minds in healthcare, "We've done all that medical science can do. We're sorry, but we can't help you." And as amazing as technology is, it alone cannot solve all matters of the body, mind, and spirit. This makes us wonder if something in the unseen world can bring us to greater wholeness now and in the life to come. This situation has set many on a quest for spirituality that has introduced them to everything from transcendental meditation to "spirituality of self" to faith healers, leading many into what I call "shadow spirituality."

Humanity, with its intense longing for wholeness, must be directed to true spirituality rooted in a daily relationship with God through His Holy Spirit and secured through the acceptance of Jesus Christ's death as the payment of the debt for our sin. In His Word, God gives us a clear standard for what it means to pursue the spirituality that brings genuine healing.

I pray that as you spend time with the Lord in this part of the devotional journey, you will experience His amazing love, the guidance of His Spirit, and the assurance that comes from a personal relationship with Jesus. As you read, study, and pray, you will put yourself in a position to experience God's healing presence through the manifestation of the fruit of the Holy Spirit.

May God bless you, and may your heart be opened to His truth as you begin the journey toward the only spirituality that will make you whole.

21

ENTER INTO HIS REST

Look around and you'll be amazed at all the manifestations of the "self" movement, including self-actualization, self-empowerment, and self-improvement. It's as if all the answers to your problems are to be found by looking within.

But this is spirituality only in the loosest sense. In truth, it's "shadow spirituality"—merely a shadow of the real thing. Shadow spirituality asks individuals to look inward, to put themselves at the center of the universe while pushing God so far to the fringes that He is left out of the picture. What remains is a spirituality of self.

In other words, shadow spirituality replaces the God of the universe with the "god within." This god is not the triune God revealed in the Bible, but rather a force that supposedly compels a person to improve himself. This god is nothing more than the human ability to learn, grow, and develop—all of which are God's gifts to people. None of these abilities, however, is capable of regenerating the human heart. Only God has that power.

The ascendance of shadow spirituality has influenced even traditional churches, and two great heresies have resulted. One is the heresy that all spirituality is good spirituality. The second is the heresy that all religions are valid as long as they promote peace and unity. Don't allow false teachers to mislead you. Instead, lay hold of the only form of spiritual power that genuinely heals you and makes you whole. It's in God's true spirituality that you find solace for your heart's deepest longings—healing for the soul, peace for the mind, and comfort for broken emotions. This healing comes only when you are committed to the pursuit of God's true spirituality.

Our nagging sense that things just aren't right can become the driving force to bring us into a personal relationship with God or bring us back to God if we have known Him but have wandered away. Because we are made in God's image, something inside tells us there is more than what we see in the physical world, more than what we can comprehend through our rational minds.

We can be pushed to the limit by the demands of modern life, leaving us weary and distraught. We are hounded by regret, we are worried, and often we are filled with anxiety. As we looked at in the first section of this devotional, discontent is a spiritual issue that requires a spiritual solution, and God alone can restore us, providing what we hunger for.

And God's deliverance and care are also what bring rest and healing to the soul.

God intended rest to be a part of the natural rhythm of life. On the seventh day of creation, the Sabbath day, our Creator rested from all His labor. He designed rest into the spiritual realm as well, holding our rest as the destination and satisfaction of our spiritual longing. Humankind's restless discontent is a search for the rest promised by the Lord, the rest that brings peace and repose to our troubled hearts. Only when our wandering leads us home to the Father will we find the peace and contentment we seek and we need for our healing.

My prayer is that you will accept God's invitation and enter into the rest that only He offers—starting in this life and continuing for eternity in the life to come. It's also my prayer that you will respond to the Holy Spirit calling you to look upward, to put God at the center of all you will face today, and to grow in understanding and in relationship with Him. Will you invite the Holy Spirit to fill you afresh this day? God has promised that He will reveal

Himself to you if you seek Him with all your heart. This is the beginning of the healing journey.

The LORD is gracious and righteous;
   our God is full of compassion.
The LORD protects the unwary;
   when I was brought low, he saved me.
Return to your rest, my soul,
   for the LORD has been good to you.

PSALM 116:5-7

Lord, I want to seek You and Your true spirituality. My faith won't grow if I know You are a healing God and still choose to look to other sources for my peace and wholeness. Guide my heart, Lord, so I know which beliefs are not of You and need to be shed from my life.

Help me seek You with my entire being. My healing and my hope are found in Your presence. Let me begin with rest. You command Your children to practice Sabbath to seek rest for Your glory and for our peace. In Your compassion and grace, You know I can't love, serve, or live a godly life when I am weary and empty. I long for the replenishment of downtime and conversation with You. I can't wait to seek renewal and the healing journey that begins and ends with You. Amen.

22

HEALING BREATH OF GOD

O ur healing God stands outside and apart from His creation. He is holy and just, and He is sovereign over all He has created. He is the omnipotent, omniscient, omnipresent One who loves us unconditionally and who desires fellowship with all humankind. But He relates to us on His terms, not on ours.

Therefore, we experience true spirituality only through God's Spirit, who indwells a person as he or she responds in faith to Jesus Christ as Savior and Lord. This is the exact opposite of shadow spirituality, which contends that the "god within" merely needs to be awakened and coaxed into actualizing activities. When the superficial, feel-good emotions are stripped away, though, one quickly realizes that New Age thinking is not new at all. It's the oldest of all philosophies, dating back to the Garden of Eden, where the first man and woman thought they could be like God. Indeed, they sought to be God.

True spirituality shows us the tragic consequences of this path. All of us are born with a missing dimension caused by the sin of wanting to live independently of God. This sin separates us from Him. The only way to fill that void is through repentance of sin, faith in Jesus Christ, and the indwelling power of God's Spirit. This is the spirituality that makes us whole. This is the spirituality that heals us.

Biblical spirituality leads us to know the light of the world, Jesus Christ, and makes it possible for us to experience wholeness of body, mind, and spirit in becoming like Him. This healing comes only as the Holy Spirit of God is invited to do His ongoing work of transformation in our lives. We are made whole when we reflect the "character-likeness" of Jesus Christ.

When God's Spirit opens our spiritual eyes, we begin to understand ourselves and recognize our own darkness and moral corruption—in other words, our sinfulness. We also wake up to the revelation that our inner longing is not a need for independence, but rather a consuming need for dependence—dependence on the Savior.

The Hebrew word for "spirit" is *ruach*, which means "breath" or "wind." One of the foremost word pictures of the Holy Spirit found in Scripture is the Breath of God. In fact, the first word picture associated with the Spirit is that of breath—of something that makes the air move, even to the point of vigorous or violent motion. It's a picture of energy released, an outward moving force of power.

As we seek to gain understanding of God's Spirit, it's important to know that the Holy Spirit desires God's best for us. He works in us individually. He convicts us of sin, glorifies Christ, leads and guides us, teaches and commands, intercedes for us, and provides divine help and care. The Holy Spirit prays through us that God's perfect will might be done in our lives.

In John 14:16, Jesus made it clear that after His resurrection, the Holy Spirit would be His personal representative on Earth. No one else is Jesus's representative—no bishop, minister, teacher, or televangelist. The Holy Spirit alone is Jesus's representative, indwelling Jesus's disciples.

The Holy Spirit is the full expression of God the Father and God the Son. Jesus said the Spirit would enable us to become more like Him. The Spirit is the fullness of God's character, love, presence, plan, and purpose.

As the Spirit does His work, He transforms us into the image of Christ Jesus.

The process of spiritual transformation brings tremendous healing to the person who previously had been ripped apart by sin. Only the Holy Spirit can renew our minds and bring us to the wholeness of spiritual transformation.

⁓

When he, the Spirit of truth, comes, he will guide you into all the truth. He will not speak on his own; he will speak only what he hears, and he will tell you what is yet to come. He will glorify me because it is from me that he will receive what he will make known to you. All that belongs to the Father is mine. That is why I said the Spirit will receive from me what he will make known to you.

JOHN 16:13-15

Lord, thank You for the gift of the Holy Spirit…Your representative who will guide and teach me. Because of Your great love and the work of the indwelling Spirit, I am being transformed into Your likeness.

My spirit is calmed and comforted by the Holy Spirit. My healing comes as I trust this "breath of God" to flow through me, to be the power that will work in me and help me to bear fruit. I long for the Holy Spirit to do Your work in me so I am shaped into the character-likeness of Jesus. May my days be a holy offering as I am made whole. Please help me to depend on Your Spirit to work in my life today. Keep my spiritual eyes open to follow Your teachings and truth. I feel Your love poured into me, Lord, and I am humbled and hopeful. Amen.

(23)

PROMISES, PROMISES

Have you lost your belief in guarantees? If you have been on this planet for a couple decades or more, you have experienced the hollowness of promises that sometimes comes attached to anything purchased or pursued in the world's arena. But God's guarantees—His promises—are never hollow. And one of those promises is this: the Holy Spirit guarantees that our status as God's own will never change. Because His seal is secure, our salvation is sure.

When we accept the sacrifice of Jesus for the remission of our sins and seek the forgiveness He made possible through His death on the cross, we receive the Holy Spirit. At that moment, the Spirit of God seals us. "You also were included in Christ when you heard the message of truth, the gospel of your salvation. When you believed, you were marked in him with a seal, the promised Holy Spirit" (Ephesians 1:13).

While the sealing of the Holy Spirit occurs only once—at the time of our surrender to Him—the filling of our lives with God's Spirit is something that can and should happen continuously. This filling is dependent upon our response to God's gracious gift of salvation and our desire to obey Jesus as our Lord. As we are filled, God's Spirit guides us, admonishes us, corrects us, comforts us, and leads us away from evil and toward the good plans and purposes of God.

While every Christian is sealed by the Holy Spirit, not every Christian chooses to be continuously filled by the Spirit. God waits for us to open ourselves to Him and yield our will to His will. It's our responsibility and privilege to invite the Holy Spirit to do His work in us and through us every day. Isn't this a great encouragement? Jesus did not leave His followers then or now without His power and wisdom. We can walk in the way of God's will because we have a personal Guide.

When the apostle Paul wrote, "Be filled with the Spirit" (Ephesians 5:18), he used a Greek verb tense that means "to be constantly or continually filled." We live in the healing power of the Holy Spirit when we are continually filled with Him. It's as if a spiritual fountain constantly flows and replenishes us. When we are filled and sated by the Spirit, we can't help but have the love of God overflow into all that we do and say. There is no end to the healing and influence of the Spirit.

If you face a healing journey of any kind, you know it can be discouraging. The pursuit of help empties us of our limited human resources in no time. Our need draws us back to the source of the Spirit over and over. And as we surrender, we will not be disappointed.

Let me be clear about the Spirit's filling. At the time of salvation, a person receives the whole of the person of the Holy Spirit, not just part of Him. But allowing Him to control our words, actions, and decisions is a daily process. We must submit every part of our lives, every day, to the Spirit's control. This includes the hardships, the needs, and the next steps in any healing journey. Have you yielded all of your life to the working of the Holy Spirit, or have you cornered His presence and power into one small area of your life?

Why don't you take time today to open up the areas of your life that have been shut off from the Holy Spirit. Open all the rooms in your heart to His healing power. Let Him break down any stronghold that might be keeping you stuck. Then give praise to God for Jesus, who made it possible for God's Spirit to dwell within you.

This is how we know that we live in him and he in us: He has given us of his Spirit.

1 JOHN 4:13

Lord, thank You for sending Your Holy Spirit, who has sealed me and who binds me to You. I praise You, God, and I thank You for the security I enjoy through Your Spirit. Each day, may I invite You to work through me and in all I do. Without this, my efforts take great labor and yield little fruit. I am amazed at what I can do when partnering with the Spirit.

Thank You, Jesus, for promising us a Comforter to dwell within us. Help me today, Father, to open my entire life to the control of Your Spirit. I want to know what it's like to end each day satisfied that I welcomed and trusted the work of the Holy Spirit. I want to go to sleep satisfied that I lived a full and righteous day that had impact on matters of eternal value. Amen.

HOLY DYNAMITE

If you needed three cups of coffee to get your morning started today, you might be a bit skeptical when I tell you that as a believer you have the mighty power of the Holy Spirit in you.

When we speak of the Holy Spirit, many people, including Christians, misunderstand the meaning of His power. They tend to define "power" as the world defines it—as an ability to control people, events, and circumstances for our own advantage. They see it as a force that can bulldoze the way clear for them to have their way. This version of power brings independence and self-sufficiency, with no need for God's help or the assistance of others.

While many devote their lives to achieving this goal, this type of power can never satisfy the soul or bring joy or peace. The world's power is temporary, leaving a person always wanting more.

In describing the power of the Holy Spirit, the Bible paints quite a different picture. The word translated as "power" in the English Bible is the Greek word *dynamis*, from which we get the word "dynamite." Jesus told His disciples that before they would be able to evangelize the world, they must receive the *dynamis* of the Holy Spirit.

The Holy Spirit possesses a dynamite-like power that works within a believer to blast out anything that is unlike God. It's not a power that exalts one person above others. It does not manipulate or control others. Instead, the Holy Spirit uses His power to break us so that He might remake us. The more we get self out of the way and yield our will to His, the more powerfully He can pour Himself through us to others, and the more powerfully He is able to transform our lives. We are merely the conduits, the channels that God's power moves through.

The Holy Spirit empowers us to be witnesses of God's love, to live in a way that pleases God, to fully meet the demands and pressures of life, and to resist temptation. If God's awesome power is available to us through the Holy Spirit, how can we tap into it? The answer is clear: We must acknowledge our utter helplessness and our complete dependence on God. The Bible tells us that God shows Himself strongest in the humblest of hearts (see James 4:6). He is able to meet every need in a life surrendered to Him alone.

We put ourselves in position to receive God's power when we become realistic about our limitations. The key to spiritual power is humility, not striving for success and seeking to promote ourselves. Whenever I am tempted to believe I'm responsible for some breakthrough in our ministry, I remember the many times I have felt overwhelmed by the demands and the difficulty of living for God. When I recall my helplessness, I grow closer to God, the Source of my strength.

As a pastor I often find myself crying, "Lord, help me. Lord, enable me. Lord, give me Your power!" I want the power of the Lord so I can witness with boldness and effectiveness. I want His power so I can live in a way that is fully pleasing to Him. I want God's power to make me equal to the demands and pressures I face and to give me victory over sin. I want God's power working in my life to defeat the spiritual enemy who seeks to bring about loss, destruction, and an end to blessings in my life.

What brings you to your knees each day to ask the Holy Spirit to blast away what is self so you can, in humility, receive His power? You don't need more coffee. You need to draw from the Source of your strength to serve and please the Lord. That is the best power breakfast this side of eternity.

***

May the God of hope fill you with all joy and peace as you trust in him, so that you may overflow with hope by the power of the Holy Spirit.

Romans 15:13

Lord, teach me about the true power of Your Spirit. I confess that You alone are God. Forgive me for the times I have wrestled with sin and hardships and not turned to the power of the Spirit. My pride has gotten in the way of my surrender to You. But I want Your dynamis to propel and transform my words, actions, and life.

Today I desire to be an open vessel for Your will and Spirit. I want to meet the demands and pressures of life and resist temptation in this power—the only power that is sufficient to win spiritual battles and fulfill Your purposes. Sometimes just getting through the day feels like a triumph, but You have much bigger hopes and victories in mind for me. May I be a witness of Your love and live in the Holy Spirit's power in a way that pleases You. Amen.

$$(25)$$

DON'T SUPPRESS THE SPIRIT

In the middle of summer, it's difficult to resist the appeal of a soft drink commercial. The beverage maker promises that drinking an ice-cold glass of their soda will quench our thirst and refresh us. We all know that a cold drink on a hot day will not make our thirst disappear forever, but it will suppress it for the moment.

The common English usage of the word "quench" might confuse us when we read, "Do not quench the Spirit" (1 Thessalonians 5:19), which warns us not to quench the Spirit of God. It's easy to assume quenching the Spirit is the same as refreshing the Spirit. However, the Greek word that is translated as quench here means to "extinguish." This word has a stronger meaning than "temporary suppression." A modern English translation says, "Do not put out the Spirit's fire" (GOD'S WORD). The same word can be used to describe the snuffing out of a candle.

By the way, this does not mean that we can permanently remove the Holy Spirit from our lives. The Spirit is indestructible in His Person and inextinguishable in His strength. Rather, quenching the Spirit means we can resist something the Holy Spirit wants to do in us or through us. It's refusing to follow His leading, ignoring His warnings and charging ahead to do things our way and in our own timing.

We all come to crossroads where we have an opportunity to yield to the Holy Spirit or to quench the Spirit's work. We may sense that we are to serve in some way, to give money to meet a need, or to change a destructive habit. To quench the Spirit is to say no to the Lord in these moments and to choose instead to pursue our own personal goals.

Are you able to identify times you have turned on a mental or spiritual fire-hose to put out the fire of the Holy Spirit instead of fanning that flame and being inspired to move forward with His leading? When we look back at these situations, we can recognize why we did this and what the consequences might be. If you held back from pursuing an opportunity to serve even though you felt led to say yes, maybe now you can identify fear as the reason you quenched the Spirit. When we are immobilized by these feelings, it's often because we don't believe the Spirit will work through us once we say yes. The consequence, sadly, is that we end up not living by the Spirit or in accordance with God's leading. We might profess a faith that is afire, but our histories will reveal a very different story...one not nearly as inspired or righteous.

Just as it's possible to disobey God even when His will for us is abundantly clear, it's also possible for us to live in such a way that the Holy Spirit withholds His power from our lives.

If we rely on our own strength, we will surely be defeated. But in the strength of the Holy Spirit, we are in a position to be more than conquerors over everything that confronts us. "In all these things we are more than conquerors through him who loved us" (Romans 8:37).

Are you tempted to take matters into your own hands and rely on your own skills and resourcefulness? Take time today to admit your inadequacies and confess your past attempts to lean on your own strength rather than rely on the power of God's Spirit.

Have you lost the power of God by putting out the Holy Spirit's fire? You can ask for forgiveness and then commit your day to Him. Ask God to help you obey the gentle voice of the Holy Spirit. Ask Him to renew His power and work within you. That is true spiritual refreshment!

⌒

Those who are led by the Spirit of God are the children of God. The Spirit you received does not make you slaves, so that you live in fear again; rather, the Spirit you received brought about your adoption to sonship. And by him we cry, "*Abba,* Father."

Romans 8:14-15

Lord, empower me afresh with Your Holy Spirit so that I might be equal to the challenges and leaps of faith You call me to make. I am sorry for the times when I have relied on my own abilities and unknowingly suppressed the power of Your Spirit. Reveal to me, in the moments of hesitation, what fears or falsehoods I am leaning on as my truth. Replace these with Your truth.

Today I ask You, Lord, to guide me as You have promised. Help me to obey the gentle voice that prompts me. I need not fear that You will orphan me when I say yes to following You. I will claim my role as a child of God who is led by the Spirit. I will not put out the fire of the Spirit, but I will fuel it with a willingness to walk in the direction You call me. Amen.

26

BEARING THE FRUIT

I f you have ever watched the harvesting of grapes, you know that two people usually work closely together. One person holds an open basket while the other cuts the grapes and lays the clusters into the container. As long as the basket carrier keeps the basket open and follows along with the cutter, her fruit basket will soon be filled to overflowing. But if she closes the basket or lags behind, she can't receive the fruit.

In a similar way, as long as you walk closely with the Lord and keep your life open to receive the daily filling of the Holy Spirit, your life will be full of the fruit of the Spirit. Your life will be overflowing.

This part of our devotional journey is about healing. We come to God as our refuge and strength for healing of our nature and our wounds. When we receive the Holy Spirit and do not quench His power, there are many gifts that fill us.

The fruit of the Spirit is character rather than conduct; it is being rather than doing. Many people mistakenly refer to the "fruits" of the Spirit. However, the fruit of the Spirit is a single fruit, not an assortment. It is the whole of God's nature imparted to us and flowing out of us as evidence that the Spirit resides in us. God's nature is not fragmented. We cannot receive just one aspect of His being. We bear all the fruit of the Spirit, not some fruit.

The apostle Paul summarized the composite nature of God's character:

> The fruit of the Spirit is love, joy, peace, forbearance, kindness, goodness, faithfulness, gentleness and self-control. Against such things there is no law. Those who belong to Christ Jesus have crucified the flesh with its passions and desires (Galatians 5:22-24).

This describes the fruit the Holy Spirit bears in our lives. What a list! Isn't this what we aspire to when we're at our most humble in God's presence?

We cannot talk ourselves into developing these character traits. We cannot study our way into them. We definitely cannot earn these attributes. They are the byproduct of our allowing the Spirit to do His work in us as we abide in the words of Christ Jesus, obey the commands of Christ, and follow the leading of the Holy Spirit. As believers who are a part of the body of Christ, we have crucified the ways of the flesh. We exchange our passions for those of God, our desires for His will. We empty ourselves of what doesn't serve the Lord, and then we are, like that basket of grapes, filled with a harvest of God's healing goodness and the power of the Spirit.

Jesus commands us to stay connected to Him, to abide in Him, to rely upon Him, and to turn to Him when facing every decision. Abiding involves becoming so connected to Him that we no longer can tell where our will ends and His begins.

When we experience the moment-by-moment filling of God's Spirit, we begin to bear the fruit of the Spirit. That's when we start to manifest the outworking of the Holy Spirit's presence. His work will transform our thoughts and emotions as well as our behavior toward others.

If you have not yet tasted the harvest of the fruit of the Spirit and witnessed its impact in your life and in the lives of those you love, care for, reach out to, and serve in Jesus's name, then get ready for an undeniable transformation.

I encourage you to keep Galatians 5:22-24 in your phone or written on something you see every day. As you abide in the Lord, you'll want to notice the fruit that is emerging from you and around you. This will be the power of the Holy Spirit at work in you, and you won't want to miss any of it.

⁓

I am the vine; you are the branches. If you remain in me and I in you, you will bear much fruit; apart from me you can do nothing.

JOHN 15:5

Lord Jesus, help me to always walk closely behind You so I can gather and exhibit the fruit of Your Spirit: love, joy, peace, patience, kindness, goodness, faithfulness, gentleness, and self-control. Restore my connection to You—the Vine—so I might bear this fruit in great measure. I want to live and give from such strength when I receive You and the power of the Spirit.

When You anointed Jesus with the Holy Spirit, He was able to heal others. The Holy Spirit did His work and changed hearts and lives. I am ready to abide in and be obedient to Jesus and follow the leading of the Holy Spirit. I want to witness the fruit of the Spirit at work through me. In this complicated world full of division, pain, and hate, I want to be a part of the healing that comes from You alone. Amen.

GOD IS LOVE

27

W e all are starving for a personal experience of genuine, biblical love. But many are going about it in an upside-down way. The teachers of shadow spirituality tell us that it's only as we love ourselves that we are able to open our hearts to receive divine love. But this is the opposite of God's true spirituality. We come to Christ when we recognize we are nothing without Him and that, even in our sinful state, Christ died for us. The person who is absorbed with self-love can't find God because he sees no need for God.

True love does not occur apart from God, and for the follower of Christ, love is not optional. That is because God's love flows from His nature. As John wrote, "Whoever does not love does not know God, because God is love" (1 John 4:8). His character is defined by love. God has made an eternal choice from the foundation of all creation that He will love His creation.

At no time does God say, "I love you whenever it's convenient." "I love you when you are good." "I love you as long as you promise to try harder." God's love is constant. It's sacrificial, aimed always at bringing about our eternal good.

God's love never varies. He loves us even when we are rebellious and disobedient, when we turn our backs on Him and refuse to return His love. He loves us. Period. He loves us because that is His choice. God is love.

Even so, we would be blind to God's awesome, unlimited, undeserved love if it weren't for the witness of the Holy Spirit. The Holy Spirit reveals that God's love was extended to us first, even when we were unworthy. The Holy Spirit also shows us that God does not require us to clean up our sinful lives before He will love us. Rather, God sent His Son to die on our behalf when we were still in full rebellion against Him.

> At just the right time, when we were still powerless, Christ died for the ungodly. Very rarely will anyone die for a righteous person, though for a good person someone might possibly dare to die. But God demonstrates his own love for us in this: While we were still sinners, Christ died for us (Romans 5:6-8).

Jesus said in the most famous verse of the New Testament, "God so loved the world that he gave his one and only Son, that whoever believes in him shall not perish but have eternal life" (John 3:16). There's nothing in that statement about our earning or being worthy of God's love. All the motivation and impetus are on God's part.

God's love drives Him to seek us out. His love always motivates Him toward us with the purpose of forgiving us, restoring us, and showering His mercy and grace upon us. This is the healing and wholeness of God's love toward us.

Our appreciation for God's love will grow when we realize that His love is not artificial or cheap. When God said to humankind, "I love you," He gave up all that was most precious to Him. He said "I love you" by paying the price for our sin, and that price was the death of His own Son. That is not a love of limits.

Comprehending this depth and breadth of love is not easy for us because we don't witness it in ourselves and others. We get glimpses of His compassion and love as we express it to one another in the body of Christ and beyond, but the purity of God's love is unmatched. And it is this love that He has for you.

Have you truly experienced God's love? Reach out to Him and open your heart to receive Him. Allow yourself to be overwhelmed with gratitude as you overflow with the unconditional love of God.

Know therefore that the LORD your God is God; he is the faithful God, keeping his covenant of love to a thousand generations of those who love him and keep his commandments.

DEUTERONOMY 7:9

God, I have been hungry for genuine, biblical love. I have had heart and head knowledge of Your love, but I have also limited how it influences my life. I've held back at times. Maybe I thought I wasn't worthy or that Your unconditional love is too good be true. But You are love. Not only does Your Word speak of Your love, the cross and the resurrection show it. And the Holy Spirit reveals it. I don't want to block its power; instead, I want to be changed, moved, and healed by its force.

Your care for Your creation will never fail or even diminish because it isn't like the world's version. You seek Your children. When I feel You pursue me, I am humbled, and my hungry heart opens to be filled. Thank You, dear Father, for caring about me so much that in Your mercy You say yes. Amen.

28

THE RESTORATIVE POWER
OF GOD'S LOVE

As a believer, you are wholly and truly loved by God. Does this sink into your spirit and influence your spiritual and emotional wellness?

Love restores us to the Father, rebuilding us from the inside out. It refashions the way we see ourselves. We are lovable because God has made us the object of His love. We are capable of loving others because God now loves others through us, and He has shown us the way. "We love because he first loved us" (1 John 4:19).

In any area in which we feel unworthy, God's love conveys, "I made you, I redeemed you, and I want you with Me forever!"

In any area in which we feel rejected, God's love says, "I have adopted you. Come, talk to Me, and spend time with Me."

In any area in which we feel shame over our sin, God's love says, "The moment you confessed and repented is the moment I forgave you. You are free of shame because of My mercy. Go and sin no more."

God's love is compelling, but He does not force us to accept it. He waits for our response. We must be ready to accept the love that He longs to shower on us through His Spirit.

Many years ago, the Holy Spirit revealed to me that I was being controlled by a life of sin. I was living under the horrors of spiritual slavery. The Holy

Spirit said to me, "I can free you! Do you want to be freed?" At first, I was reluctant to turn from my old way of life. *If I break free of this bondage,* I reasoned, *I might miss out on the good things that I can get from my slave master.*

Here is what the Holy Spirit showed me: "Your slave master [Satan] tells you lies so that you will believe that he always will have you under his control." Then the Holy Spirit asked me, "Is that what you want?"

My answer was a resounding no!

Then God's Spirit graciously said, "Let me introduce you to Jesus. He has already rendered Satan ineffective. Jesus loves you with immeasurable, incomprehensible, unconditional love. He died for you even when you preferred to hang out with your slave master, and now He invites you to experience all the riches He has in store for you."

The Holy Spirit showed me through the eyes of faith what my future with this loving Savior would be like. He opened my eyes to the glories, joys, and blessedness of heaven. By this time I was crying out, "Save me from my slave master! Release me from my sin and guilt and bondage." And in Jesus's great love, He did just that.

As long as we are relying on our own strength to get through life, we won't recognize our need for the comfort of God's love. But when we feel deep remorse over our sin and our failure to trust in God, that's when we realize our need for the forgiving mercy of God's love. Sin keeps us from God's love, but seeking God's forgiveness restores us to Him. If we stay stuck in shame rather than taking our sin to God, we miss out on His healing.

As you rest in God's forgiveness, don't allow the sin of unforgiveness to keep you estranged from another person. Reach out to that person with forgiveness and love. Not only will you be healed in the process, but others will find themselves in position to be healed as well. Let the healing power of God's love restore your own life and allow God to use you to bring His healing love to others. You can fully love others because He first loved you.

Embrace God's grace instead of the doubts in your head and ask God to reveal the healing power of His love to you.

⌒

This is what the LORD says—
>he who created you, Jacob,
>he who formed you, Israel:
"Do not fear, for I have redeemed you;
>I have summoned you by name; you are mine."

ISAIAH 43:1

Lord, help me let go of my selfish agenda and open myself fully to Your love. When I focus on my thoughts or on difficult circumstances, I lean into my shortcomings. It's difficult to come to You with a hearty belief that Your love will reach me and cover me with all my failings. When I feel unworthy, rejected, or full of shame, Your voice, Your Word comfort me and remind me that I am Your beloved child. You made me worthy. And You made me love You and be loved by You.

Help me trust in Your compelling grace. I don't stand on the sinking sand of my circumstances or negative thoughts, I stand on the strong foundation of mercy, forgiveness, and redemption. I will approach my day empowered by these truths. I stand before You humbled and in need...and yet worthy and ready for Your healing love. Amen.

(29)

PROTECTING OUR JOY

Would the people in your life think of you as a joyful person?

Years ago someone noted that the best argument for Christianity is a Christian who is joyful, certain of his faith, and complete in his character. Likewise, one of the strongest arguments against Christianity is a believer who is somber and joyless, self-righteous, and smug, feeling complacent in his consecrated state.

Joy—mentioned 70 times in the New Testament—is essential to the Christian life. Yet as much as we value it, many of us fail to connect our faith with God's joy. Some Christians even think that Sunday morning is a time to be somber. My friend, take this to heart: True spirituality finds true expression in the joy of the Lord!

As we abide in the knowledge that Jesus is our Savior and the Lord of our lives, the Holy Spirit is free to manifest the character trait of joy in our lives. "If you keep my commands, you will remain in my love, just as I have kept my Father's commands and remain in his love. I have told you this so that my joy may be in you and that your joy may be complete" (John 15:10-11).

We want that joy to be complete in us, don't we? And yet it's easy to fall under the influence of the biggest culprits in undermining our experience of joy: jealousy and envy.

Jealousy and envy are works of the flesh that wage war against the spirit and destroy your joy. In order to protect your joy, you must learn to recognize them and distinguish between the two.

Jealousy is a passionate desire to hold on to something that is already yours. The Lord God is described as being "jealous" for His people—He desires to keep them close to Himself. This is the legitimate, protective feeling the Lord has regarding something that rightfully belongs to Him.

However, on a human scale, jealousy can consume us. Extremely jealous people experience great anxiety as they cling tightly to everything in an attempt to prevent others from winning away what they feel is rightfully theirs. Can you identify a particular area of jealousy in your life right now? How has it compromised your joy and contentment?

Envy is a bit different. Many people who seem to have everything still envy the possessions of others. Envy is the desire to have more than you already have, and it will incapacitate you. Proverbs 14:30 says, "A heart at peace gives life to the body, but envy rots the bones."

This is so prevalent today. We are bombarded with images and information about the successes, possessions, and even relationships of others, particularly on social media. The impulse to compare and then complain is strong. We think, *That should be mine. Why don't I have that in my life?* Envy can turn our hearts against God because we doubt God's sufficiency and His plan for us.

The apostle Paul found that contentment is the only solution to bone-rotting envy. Contentment with what we have, what we don't have, and in whatever circumstances we are in because we are in the care and love of the Lord. Things of the world and not of God should never dictate your contentment or joy because they are temporal and come and go. The love of God remains steadfast!

In the end, both jealousy and envy involve a preoccupation with what we want to control or possess. It's a losing battle with the biggest losses being your joy and peace in God. Who wants to sacrifice that? Examine your heart carefully. Are you harboring feelings of jealousy or envy? If so, confess that to God and surrender them gladly. With these feelings regularly removed from your heart, you will be free to experience the power, blessing, contentment, and healing of God's joy.

<hr>

I have learned to be content whatever the circumstances. I know what it is to be in need, and I know what it is to have plenty. I have learned the secret of being content in any and every situation, whether well fed or hungry, whether living in plenty or in want.

PHILIPPIANS 4:11-12

Lord, I want to be a believer who shows the joy that comes from You. Let Your love rule in my heart so that envy and jealousy do not steal the joy You provide. When I find myself wasting energy and time protecting what I have or wishing I had what others possess, may I remember what matters. Keep me, Father, from investing my life in things that are temporal. They don't promise joy or contentment. They promise a constant desire for more of me and more of the world, but not more of You.

Lord, I can be content because I know You alone are good and I lack nothing. I will fix my eyes on You and prepare my heart with gratitude to be filled by You alone. May Your joy be in me and my joy be made complete because of You. Amen.

30

TRUE SPIRITUAL JOY

The best way to experience the joy of the Holy Spirit is to stop what you are doing and park yourself in God's presence. Sit quietly and allow your mind and heart to rest in His sufficiency while the Lord assures you afresh that you are the recipient of His grace and mercy, not only today but always.

To truly benefit from the healing power of joy, we must understand some important truths.

Joy is not the same as happiness. The world's obsession with happiness is often confused with spiritual joy. The world may speak about joy while thinking about candy (Almond Joy), a computer game accessory (joystick), or going for an unauthorized trip in a fast car (joyride). But each of these is nothing more than a moment of temporary, fleeting pleasure.

One of the main distinctions between joy and happiness is that joy is an abiding quality while happiness is a temporary emotion. Happiness is rooted in favorable circumstances and enjoyable activities. Because it's dependent on external conditions, happiness can never be fully satisfied.

True spiritual joy comes from the inside. It doesn't come from favorable economic conditions, being accepted by society, or owning a luxury car. Joy comes from one thing only: a sure knowledge that you are saved through the death and the resurrection of the Lord Jesus Christ. Real joy comes from knowing that your sins are forgiven, that God is working all things together for your eternal good, and that He is preparing an eternal home for you.

Joy is not the absence of adversity or pain and sorrow. Joy flourishes in the lives of those who pursue true spirituality even in the face of trouble. From a prison cell, Paul wrote to the Philippians, "Rejoice in the Lord always. I will say it again: Rejoice!" (Philippians 4:4).

Joy is rooted in the sure knowledge that God is with us in our pain and sorrow and that absolutely nothing can separate us from His love (see Romans 8:38-39). God is at work on our behalf whether we are employed or unemployed, embraced or rejected by others, criticized or praised.

Do you have a deep, abiding sense of His love and presence that satisfies and assures you even when things are not going as planned or desired?

Joy is not the denial of reality. Some people believe that joy amid pain and sorrow is nothing more than a refusal to acknowledge the reality of difficulties. God's Word never requires us to deny reality; rather, we are to confront reality with faith, live above the moment, and see the future God holds out to us.

When you are in a season of lack and can experience and express the joy of the Lord, you don't have your head in the sand. You have your mind and heart in the heavens. That's not denial...it's eternal perspective.

Joy is not based on having things under control. Countless people believe they will have joy if they can just get past their current crisis, pay their current bills, meet their current deadlines. These expectations are doomed to failure because joy is not the result of our striving. Joy is the result of letting go of anxiety and trusting God to do His work in us and on our behalf.

Joy is healing! Your joy will come because of trusting God to walk with you through the difficult times as He works behind the scenes to bring about blessing. The joy of the Lord gives you strength and heals you.

Have you wasted weeks or even months striving to gain control in your life? Have you agonized during times of trial or uncertainty as you tried to fix the situation? Take a moment to sit in silence before the Lord to allow the healing power of His joy to cover you.

Satisfy us in the morning with your unfailing love,
     that we may sing for joy and be glad all our days.

Psalm 90:14

Dear Father, when I embrace joy, I know I'm not signing up to have a perfect life with zero problems. I am welcoming Your healing and Your hope into my life. And when trouble comes, I can rest in the security of Your presence because You are faithful.

I want to know Your joy more than I want to taste the fleeting pleasure of happiness. The shiny things that appeal to me in the world will, once attained, leave me disappointed and discouraged. I become jaded by the false promises that bombard me daily. Help me abide in Your sure promise, Lord. You satisfy the soul, and Your Word is never hollow or false. In fact, the more I know of You, and the more I invest in the pursuit of Your heart, the more joy I feel. I praise You today for the gift of Your unfailing love. Amen.

31

MENDING A TROUBLED HEART

What steals our peace? That question may cause us to envision lists of worries that keep us up at night. While our lists may be different, Jesus helps us all understand what is beneath the unrest and where our peace lies.

"Peace I leave with you; my peace I give you. I do not give to you as the world gives. Do not let your hearts be troubled and do not be afraid" (John 14:27). Jesus described the root causes of worry and anxiety, which for all of us are fear and a troubled heart.

Fear is the great foe of peace, and it comes in many guises, including panic, dread, and worry. Getting to the core of the fear that lies behind many other emotions is like peeling away layers of old wallpaper. You recognize regret, and underneath it you uncover self-centeredness. You peel back self-centeredness, and you find doubt. You peel back doubt, and you find fear. Fear, ultimately, is a lack of trust in God.

We struggle with a fear of failure, sickness, bad outcomes for our children, and what will happen to us if we make this decision or that. In some cases, it's a nagging fear that cannot be readily defined. Other times, the fear brings about the thing we fear most. We fear rejection, so we avoid reaching out to others and become isolated. This causes us to appear arrogant or uninterested, and soon others avoid us. We can set in motion a fulfillment of some fears all because we didn't first seek God's peace.

Our hearts also become troubled by anxiety—a close cousin of fear—which causes us to be preoccupied by a circumstance and possibly led by false reasoning that if things were resolved, life would be great. We tell ourselves, "If I only had X number of dollars in the bank, then I could stop worrying." The truth is that financial security is powerless to deliver peace of mind because earthly riches are temporary.

We can grow anxious over an encounter with the general sinfulness of humankind. Sin interrupts our peace by causing shame and worry. Or we are injured by another's sinful behavior, causing us to feel pain, powerlessness, and anger. The result is a loss of peace for both parties.

Anytime we allow a problem to loom larger than God, we are prone to fear and anxiety. The greater our fear grows, the less we're able to see God beyond the problem. The solution is not to deny the problem but to run to the Source of peace.

Take your mind off the problem by focusing on God. Meditate on His goodness and His greatness. Fear is self-focused, but peace comes through centering our minds and hearts on who God is. Faith in our heavenly Father replaces the anxiety of our what-if questions with great assurance. God is in control of all things, including every detail and circumstance of our lives and our deaths. Therefore, we can rest in that knowledge and experience His peace.

What are you most afraid of? Failure, loss, potential tragedy? No matter what it is, you can be certain that Jesus conquered all these things at the cross. Ask Him to fill your heart and calm your mind with His supernatural peace. What is your anxiety level? Are you suppressing feelings of worry or dread? The peace God offers is more powerful than all your emotions. Ask Him to show you the amazing benefits of living under the shelter of His peace.

The next time you're tempted to sift through that mental list...stop. Place those concerns, anxieties, and fears into the hands of Christ. In Him, our future is secure—both on earth and in eternity. This is the spiritual truth that calms anxiety, removes fear, and mends our troubled hearts, freeing us to live fully, abundantly in God's great peace.

"Though the mountains be shaken
and the hills be removed,
yet my unfailing love for you will not be shaken
nor my covenant of peace be removed,"
says the LORD, who has compassion on you.

ISAIAH 54:10

Lord, I submit my fear to You. In faith, I claim Your promises and Your peace. I know that You, Father, are bigger than anything that stresses me. When I start to worry over things I can't control, stop me. Shift my attention to You and Your strength. The world could crumble around me, but Your love is unchanging, and Your peace cannot be taken from me. My list of worries, anxieties, and layered fears is nothing compared to Your compassion and promises.

Help me trust You without allowing anxiety to overcome my thoughts. May I hand my concerns over to You daily so my mind and spirit are calm. In Your presence I find shelter and protection. I hope to stand in Your peace with confidence before I let anticipated problems and fears have momentum. I want to enjoy the security and healing of Your peace. Amen.

32

GOD'S POSSIBILITIES

We can take the pulse of our peace in God by looking at how we respond to situations. When you face a challenge or sense God calling you forward, which is activated first—your fear or your faith? Every time I read about a biblical character who lacked peace, I see fear. And every time I see fear, I notice that faith is lacking.

Even as regular churchgoing believers, we may hesitate to embrace our faith when we face small and big battles. We have tension in relationships, we are challenged by illnesses or deaths of people we love, or we encounter our own immortality. Sometimes all it takes is one phone call or one bill that shakes our sense of security in God's presence.

When peace is not in us or cultivated through a consistent trust in the Lord, it won't be our first response. And healing won't come if we remain entrenched in fear.

What do we do? How do we surrender the fear and become an open vessel for God's peace? Our faith is activated when we say to Jesus, "I know You are the answer to all of my needs and the solution to all of my problems. I believe—help any unbelief that remains in me to be turned into belief."

This is the path to God's peace amid the troubles of life. Faith opens us up to the healing power and transformation of "God possibilities." God can do all things, and He will open a way where there seems to be no way. Faith causes us to cling to God's promise that a bright future lies ahead. And even if that future is not experienced on earth, It most assuredly will be experienced in heaven.

Faith is the direct path to God's healing peace, which comes to us in "radiant circles." First, we experience the peace of God in our hearts and minds. Our emotions and our spirits are settled, at rest—regardless of the turmoil raging around us. As our minds and hearts become calm, we are more open to God's wisdom. That is when a clearer awareness of our problems emerges as well as a clearer awareness of God's intervention and answers to those problems.

A second realm of peace has to do with our outward behavior. The person who feels God's peace cannot help but act in a way that reflects the peace of God. What is inside the person manifests itself in body language, expression, speech, and other forms of behavior toward others. The person of peace becomes a calming presence who leads by example and reveals that there is a way to respond that is life giving and trust building. They lead others to the Source of peace. Then as the circles of peace radiate outward, those who follow God will resolve their problems with the peace of God reigning in their hearts. When others observe this, they very often seek to align themselves with these calm and wise problem solvers. God's peace, active in our lives, draws others to God.

A noticeable shift takes place when you surrender to and exhibit the fruit of the Spirit—you become a person who thinks in terms of what is possible with God. You are not limited by what is impossible to do or believe in your own ability and character. Instead of feeling frozen by fear, you will be empowered by this possibility.

Will you allow God's perfect peace to free your mind from all that troubles you? Place your trust in God and invite His peace to wash over you. When you are buoyed by His love and gentle guidance, give praise to Jesus, the Prince of Peace.

The mind governed by the flesh is death, but the mind governed by the Spirit is life and peace.

ROMANS 8:6

Lord, please give me the faith to trust You in every circumstance. I want to respond to anything and everything from a place of faith, not fear. Help me in my unbelief. I feel ashamed at how quickly I can let go of the lifeline of faith and be shut down by fear. I see how it limits me and the work You do through me. I don't want regrets later about how I have lived my life.

I trust You, Lord, and I want my words, actions, and choices to show this. I want my love for others to be fearless and my love for You to be evident. Guide me to those who are filled with Your peace so I can draw inspiration from their example. I pray to show up for others as a faithful presence that reduces strife, brings calm, and points to You. Amen.

$$\binom{33}{}$$

PAUSE BEFORE IMPATIENCE

Not long ago I went to a bookstore to find a book on patience, but I came away empty-handed. Patience is something most people want, but it's not a popular book topic or conversation starter. Exploring it makes us uncomfortable because few of us have developed and maintained patience as a practice and as fruit of the Spirit. Even Christians want instant answers to prayer, quick holiness, ready-made spiritual maturity, and miracles on demand.

I have to remind myself that God took six months to reveal to Noah the best parking place for the ark! If you struggle with patience as I do, look with me at the most common causes of a lack of patience.

A narrow worldview. Sometimes a person focuses only on their own needs and their own little world. Impatience is manifested when his needs go unmet, his schedule is interrupted, or his views are challenged.

A need for visible evidence. We become impatient when we insist on concrete proof that things are improving. We forget that God is always at work on our behalf even when we don't sense that things are going the way we want them to. True spirituality produces patience that springs from the expectancy that God cares about every detail of our lives, with or without visible evidence.

Unrealistic expectations. Impatience arises when we expect others to function just as we do. We need to develop realistic expectations, allowing others the freedom to be who God made them to be. Developing empathy for others expands our capacity to be patient with their efforts and their growth even when their pace and direction differ from our own.

Out-of-balance priorities. When we make the wrong things high priorities, we become impatient. But when God is at the center of our lives, our priorities will fall into place, and we'll find greater patience with life circumstances. The patient person continues in faith until God accomplishes His will in her and through her.

When you encounter these potential triggers, do you pause to approach them with patience, or does your impatience increase? In cartoons, impatience has been shown as an explosive device with a short, lit fuse. This is an apt visual. Impatience is marked by many emotions, and sometimes they are volatile. Chief among them are frustration and feelings of being frantic or out of control. At the root of impatience, however, is anger.

The Greek word that is translated as "patience," *makrothumia,* is made up of two words. The first half of the Greek word means "anger," which includes frustration. The second half means either "long in coming" or "slow in appearing." Patience, then, is anger that is delayed and frustration that is postponed.

The opposite of patience is a quickness to become angry. When someone speaks to us rudely or cuts us off in traffic, we experience an outburst of spontaneous anger or a quick eruption of frustration. An equally unhealthy response would be to suppress our feelings of anger. This anger is stone faced and silent. But suppressed anger doesn't disappear; instead, it goes underground, where it can fester and one day erupt like a volcano. Holding anger inside hardens the heart and limits flexibility or forgiveness toward others. I know people who have held on to anger since early in life. Anger becomes an anchor that limits us, binds us, and restricts us from moving forward in our healing and purpose.

But there is good news for us. The Lord describes Himself as being slow to anger. God's patience brings healing both to hotheads and to those who habitually suppress their anger. The solution that God's Spirit brings is the "long in coming" ability to express anger positively and appropriately, coupled with the willingness to wait for God to do His work in us.

The LORD, the LORD, the compassionate and gracious God, slow to anger, abounding in love and faithfulness, maintaining love to thousands, and forgiving wickedness, rebellion and sin.

EXODUS 34:6-7

Lord, I am grateful that You are slow to anger. Teach me to be patient with the people and the circumstances in my life. I can look to Your character and rest in Your love and gentleness when I encounter times of strong emotion. When impatience stirs anger, instill in me Your peace. How many times have You waited for me to come to You with my struggles or to do the right thing? Help me to extend grace to others. You know their hearts and what You have planned for them—I don't. I want to be an encourager and not an obstacle in my progress as a person of patience.

Forgive my impatience with You when waiting for guidance. Even in the waiting, I trust You and Your care. Thank You for never leaving me alone in the waiting. Amen.

34

WAITING IN FAITH

Waiting is not easy. And waiting on the Lord can sometimes be downright painful when we don't know what is coming, what He will ask of us, or how a situation will unfold. But God does. We're partnering with Him in obedience when we don't second-guess something He has started in us or in the world around us.

If you have followed a prompt from God and stepped onto a path without assurances of where it is leading, you know what it is to be patient. You also likely know what it feels like to push aside fear and doubt to remain committed.

No matter where we find ourselves and what questions may arise from within us or from the people around us, our faithfulness shows in how we respond to the waiting and the unknowing. When we don't see an immediate turnaround from evil to good, yet we persevere in standing up for God's righteousness, we are demonstrating the fruit of the Spirit. When everyone around us is taking shortcuts and we choose instead to do the right thing, we are manifesting the fruit of the Spirit.

Patience is an act of faith and ultimately is our expression of trust in the Lord. When we partner with Him in the waiting, we do so because we choose to believe in the hope of things to come. He'll come through as will His provision, guidance, plan, and care. Looking back at examples of His faithfulness in the Bible or in your personal life is a great way to reinforce your patience and ability to wait. And wait. And maybe wait some more.

Such surrender to and anticipation of God's follow-through is not only about us. We glorify God when we are long-suffering toward those who wrong us. We glorify Him when we are long-suffering in our actions to confront sin and evil, and when we are patient but steadfast in our refusal to give in to temptation. It's then that we are manifesting the spiritual fruit of patience.

We cannot do this alone. There is no way we can generate this kind of long-suffering spirit apart from the Spirit of God. It's not within our capacity to be this patient. It's when the Spirit of God is pouring patience into our hearts that patience becomes something we are, not simply something we do. God is patience through us.

Godly patience puts you in a position to do things on God's timetable, based on His deadlines. If God has directed you to perform a certain task or to carry out a particular ministry, then immediately do what God is calling you to do. If you think you don't have the time, then reevaluate the demands that originate with you or with those around you. Those things in the majority of cases do not require your immediate attention. But God's leading in your life deserves your immediate compliance.

When we slow down and ask God to fill us with His patience, He will help us see what is truly important. Then we will discover the rhythm of activity that He desires for us and the timetable He has set for us. When we manifest the patience of the Holy Spirit, we become partners in the process of God's revealing Himself to others through us. And in this process, we will find that God is healing our lives day by day.

If you are tired of trying to be patient in your own strength, admit your exhaustion to the Lord. Then allow His Spirit to fill you with His long-suffering patience. The Lord sent His Holy Spirit to comfort you at all times, including times of waiting. Though for a while God may be silent, His Spirit is always with you, and an answer will come in His perfect timing.

⌒

We wait in hope for the LORD;
    he is our help and our shield.
In him our hearts rejoice,
    for we trust in his holy name.

PSALM 33:20-21

Lord, I confess my weariness while waiting on You and persevering in my circumstances. I want to live and respond to others from the well of spiritual hope and faith, trust and joy. Please help me manifest Your long-suffering. Hold me back from responding with fear or expressing a first reaction that is fueled by stress, not peace. Sometimes I feel as though I'm living in a pressure cooker, but now I realize that much of the pressure is from within. You show me what to prioritize, and You remind me that doing all the things or being all the things immediately is a message from the world, not from You.

I praise You for Your infinite, intricate care. I'm thankful for the release valves of prayer and reading Your promises. When I focus on partnering with You and wait for Your wisdom and timing to prevail, I can breathe again. Amen.

35

KINDNESS AS CHARACTER

I t's easier to win over someone with sugar than with salt." You probably know this expression or a version of it. The message is that using kindness and sweetness will get you further toward what you want than if you take a harsher, less palatable approach. While this can be true, if we view kindness only in this limited and self-serving way, we miss out on its power as the fruit of the Spirit, and we underestimate how transforming an act of kindness is for both the giver and the recipient.

Too many people see kindness toward others as a nice option rather than as an essential reflection of the character of God. People show kindness if they happen to be in the right mood, or if being kind can serve their own purposes (back to the sugar scenario). But the kindness we read about in the Bible is not determined by convenience or personal preference. It's a vital characteristic of our lived-out faith because it's a vital characteristic of God's nature.

God's revelation of Himself to humankind is based on His kindness. It was out of kindness that God made a covenant with Israel and that He kept His side of the covenant despite the blatant disobedience of His people. It was out of kindness that God left the splendor and majesty of heaven and chose to hang on a criminal's cross to pay the wages of sin for all who might believe in Him. It is out of kindness that God accepts repentant sinners.

Manifesting the kindness of God's Spirit is not a hit-or-miss process of doing nice things. Instead, it's characterized by traits that are clearly defined in the Bible.

First, Spirit-endued kindness gives us the ability to empathize with others by putting ourselves in their place. Too many of us forget what we experienced in an earlier stage of life or during a time of great difficulty. Rigidity and lack of sympathy are by-products of forgetting our own shortcomings. The kind person has a way of remembering times of difficulty or confusion and can then empathize with others in their weaknesses. Kindness compels us to reach out to the person struggling with sin and speak words that bring about repentance and forgiveness.

Second, the person who manifests Spirit-endued kindness can show kindness to himself. This is not self-indulgent but rather merciful because it allows a person to let go of his or her past sin and say, "I will not beat myself up over sin God has already forgiven." Instead of punishing himself for his own forgiven sins, the apostle Paul said, "Forgetting what is behind and straining toward what is ahead, I press on toward the goal" of pursuing Christ and of being Christ's witness (Philippians 3:13-14). He understood that to be used by God, he had to accept God's grace and move forward in it.

Third, the person who manifests this fruit of the Spirit can receive the kind expressions of others. For years I struggled with this. I could easily, happily show kindness and grace to others, but I was uncomfortable receiving it from people. Then a friend and mentor said to me, "When you refuse to accept the kindness of others, you are depriving them of the joy of showing kindness." Now I find myself more willing to be a recipient because I want others to experience more of God's joy in their lives! As it turns out, giving *and* receiving kindness graciously is ministry.

Fourth, the person who manifests the kindness of God is willing to let go of hatred, bitterness, and resentment. A person cannot manifest genuine kindness and allow an imaginary war of he-said/I-said and she-did/I-did scenarios to rage in her heart.

Allow the power of the Holy Spirit to grow kindness in your spirit so that it influences how you accept God's love and show it to others. May it overflow.

⌒

You gave me life and showed me kindness,
   and in your providence watched over my spirit.

JOB 10:12

Lord, help me empty myself of resentment and bitterness so I can grow in Your kindness and show kindness to others. Soften and expand my heart so that I do not allow hardships to harden my ability to bear the fruit of the Spirit. Father, show me the way of empathy toward others so that I will live out the mercy You model to me daily.

Because of Your kindness, I am saved as a believer, and I know what it is to be cared for without condition. Like Paul, I will choose to accept Your kindness and grace so that I will not limit the Spirit's work in my life. Increase my ability to receive kindness from others as an extension of Your provision and love. There is relief in letting down the walls within me so kindness can be taken in and kindness can pour forth and do Your healing work in others. Amen.

36

THE BALM OF KINDNESS

W hen has someone's kindness amazed you or challenged you? If you haven't witnessed such an example personally, you can turn to Scripture, where we have an elevated example—one that I admit challenges and inspires me every time I read it.

In chapter 10 of the book of Luke, Jesus tells a story that opens our eyes to many essential principles about kindness. A man was going down from Jerusalem to Jericho when he fell into the hands of robbers. They stripped him of his clothes, beat him, and went away, leaving him half dead.

But a Samaritan came to where the man was, and when he saw him, he took pity on him. He went to him and bandaged his wounds, pouring on oil and wine. Then he put the man on his donkey, took him to an inn, and took care of him. The next day he took out two silver coins and gave them to the innkeeper.

"Look after him," he said, "and when I return, I will reimburse you for any extra expense you may have" (Luke 10:35).

Who was healed in this story? Certainly, the man who had fallen victim to robbers. But by extending this kindness, the Samaritan also brought about a broader healing. He broke down barriers of prejudice between Samaritans and Jews. Kindness across all boundaries can heal the suspicion and hatred that build up and eat away at entire groups of people. Maybe every generation

claims this, but at this time in our world, we desperately need this healing
kindness between groups, communities, neighbors, strangers, and even family
members. There are differences that may seem insurmountable, and yet God's
kindness—kindness as fruit of the Spirit—can rise above chasms and become
a bridge that unites. Do all divides cease? No. But through the act of being
a kind human, we usher in the supernatural healing of God to bring about
restoration. We can break our current society's unspoken and spoken rules of
not engaging with someone who thinks and lives differently than we do and
embrace God's rules of loving thy neighbor.

God's kindness heals hatred. You cannot show kindness to a person and
continue to hate him. You cannot pray for a person, believing that God will act
kindly on her behalf, and continue to resent her. But kindness doesn't stop at
healing relationships. It also has clear personal health benefits. Hatred, bitterness,
and resentment create unease that eats away at the soul. Countless diseases—
both physical and emotional—have been associated with harboring bitterness.

Kindness opens your soul to the balm of Christ's healing presence. It makes
room for love to take root. Consider how, in your life now, you can set aside
your agenda and your fear of rejection and manifest the kindness of the Holy
Spirit. What might this look like? How could a tension or divide be healed?

In a world where shadow spirituality regards self-promotion as a virtue, true
spirituality calls us to bear the fruit of kindness. Kindness is a turning of self
inside out to give to others, not only of our material resources, but also our
time, presence, and attention. Kindness occurs as a by-product of our being
filled daily with the Spirit of God and seeking to manifest His life in the world.

God's true spirituality calls us to take no thought for ourselves but to seek
the good of others. We are not to be motivated by the reward a good deed may
bring, but rather by how a good deed might help another person and transform the circumstances as well as the hearts involved.

What type of healing can God's kindness bring to your life? Will relationships be restored? Will your emotional or physical health be improved? Ask

the Holy Spirit to fill you afresh today so you can experience the healing power of God's kindness.

Get rid of all bitterness, rage and anger, brawling and slander, along with every form of malice. Be kind and compassionate to one another, forgiving each other, just as in Christ God forgave you.

EPHESIANS 4:31

Praise You, God, for Your kindness. I need and want to help share its healing power. Lord, You know the person I struggle extending kindness toward. Release me from my bitterness and my rigid and self-protective ways. Remind me that the kindness that flows to this person and situation is from You. It's beyond me and bigger than my human efforts.

When I look the other way because I don't want to be vulnerable or am afraid to be the first to move toward kindness, empathy, and sacrificial service, empower me to act as Your hands and heart. I want to be like the Samaritan—willing to go the extra mile, cross society's boundaries, and share the balm of kindness with the oppressed. I need this healing, and so does my community. I prepare my heart now in prayer to live from the source of Your unconditional kindness and forgiveness. Amen.

37

GREAT IS HIS GOODNESS

I know you have tried—we all have—but despite our best human efforts, we simply can't be good without God. The path of goodness is closed to us unless He constantly fills us with true spirituality. And when He does, friend, big changes follow. The goodness of God promotes wholeness in a person. Unlike evil, which is fragmented and can work at odds with itself, God's goodness is always unified, and it impacts all areas of life. Here is how the Holy Spirit works in us to accomplish His goodness.

Goodness causes us to focus on what is good. The apostle Paul wrote about this to the Philippians: "Whatever is true, whatever is noble, whatever is right, whatever is pure, whatever is lovely, whatever is admirable—if anything is excellent or praiseworthy—think about such things" (Philippians 4:8). We are to capture our thoughts, turning them toward the goodness of God. Our actions and responses follow as we focus on what is good. We don't seek out conflict in situations, but, rather, we look for the good and pray for God's leading in this direction.

Goodness changes the way we speak. Certainly, one who manifests the goodness of God's Spirit will not engage in cursing, bigoted jokes, or gossip. But goodness also fills our mouths with encouraging words that build up others. We lose some language and gain life-giving words. Spend time this week observing how you speak to yourself and to your family. What simple word changes could increase wellness and connection? Guide hearts toward God's goodness by being quick to praise Him and eager to speak His hope into others.

Goodness affects our behavior toward others. As we focus on God's goodness, our emotional responses to others will change. When we respond in anger or bitterness—or when we undercut or defame others—we are trying to keep them at a distance. Jesus taught the opposite approach, which calls us to step closer. "Love your enemies, do good to those who hate you, bless those who curse you, pray for those who mistreat you. If someone slaps you on one cheek, turn to them the other also. If someone takes your coat, do not withhold your shirt from them" (Luke 6:27-29).

What a high standard Jesus set! High but entirely doable in the power of the Holy Spirit. When we do good to those who have harmed or angered us, the other person's hatred is defused. Most people who have willfully caused pain are unsettled by a response of goodness and peace. Also, the Spirit-led response of goodness touches those who surround the wrongdoer. The actions of goodness lead them to question, "What purpose is there in pursuing hatred?"

Goodness challenges us to see another's actions in a new light. The harm that another person commits is not only against us, but also against God. Deep inside, the person is most likely reacting against the reflection of God at work in our lives. They hate that we stand up for a truth they have rejected. So when they respond harshly and passionately, we must see that they are lashing out at God, not at us.

The Holy Spirit leads us to ask, "If this person were to speak to Jesus this way, how would Jesus respond?" We know Jesus would speak loving words. They may be firm words of gentle rebuke, but they would be loving, nonetheless. As we seek to emulate Jesus, the Holy Spirit empowers us to do good to a person who has hurt us.

When we express the spiritual fruit of goodness, we provide an opportunity for the Holy Spirit to work in another person's life as well as our own. Ask to be filled with the desire to respond to others in this manner—you'll witness how the positive spiritual impact multiplies on Earth and glorifies God in heaven.

⌇

Make every effort to add to your faith goodness; and to goodness, knowledge; and to knowledge, self-control; and to self-control, perseverance; and to perseverance, godliness; and to godliness, mutual affection; and to mutual affection, love.

2 PETER 1:5-7

Lord, I turn my focus to Your goodness. The news of the world and the uncertainties in my life can keep me mired in a language of loss and fear. I want a vocabulary of faith and belief to replace those tired terms of despair. I don't want false cheer. I want godly goodness to fill me and overflow to others including my family, coworkers, and people I meet. A kind word and sincere gesture of Your goodness can transform a day, a heart, a life.

I ask for the honor of becoming an instrument of Your love for someone who is unaware of Your saving grace. I will watch for opportunities to manifest Your goodness toward others through my words, actions, thoughts, and responses. Let compassion fill my heart so I instinctively approach everyone with tenderness rather than judgement. Your goodness is meant to be proclaimed and shared. Amen.

38

TAKING GOD AT HIS WORD

D o I have your word?" When is the last time you said this to conclude a business meeting, retail purchase, or conversation? Gone are the days when we seek a person's word as their bond of loyalty or honor. Are we cynical or just scared to trust?

Likewise, "faithfulness" has all but fallen out of circulation. The word "faithful" is far more likely to be ascribed to a favorite pet than to a spouse. And on the rare occasion when it is associated with a person, it more likely refers to a faithful friend than a faithful God.

But evidence of God's faithfulness is all around us. God always loves. He always forgives repentant sinners. He always accomplishes His plans and fulfills His purposes.

Jesus's disciples knew they could count on Him. Every time they were in danger or need, He was there for them. He came to His disciples with words of comfort and assurance, even if doing so meant walking on water or appearing suddenly inside a locked room. His faithfulness extends even to His walking out of a sealed and heavily guarded tomb.

Just as Jesus can be counted on to keep His word, the Holy Spirit is faithful to us. Jesus said of the Spirit:

> I will ask the Father, and he will give you another advocate to help you and be with you forever—the Spirit of truth. The world cannot accept him, because it neither sees him nor knows him. But you know him, for he lives with you and will be in you. I will not leave you as orphans; I will come to you (John 14:16-18).

The Holy Spirit is always present with us. Faithfulness produces a deep assurance that we are connected to God with a bond that cannot be broken. The person who lives with this kind of assurance has a deep and abiding confidence that cannot be shaken.

Faithfulness also births a deep knowledge that what we say and do under the guidance of the Holy Spirit will yield a harvest in God's kingdom. Faithfulness forms a security that manifests itself in confidence and strength of character. It's rooted in trust, which is produced when we make a commitment and then honor it. When we say something and mean it.

God's faithfulness to us leads to our faithfulness to Him and to others. This fruit of the Spirit grows and, ultimately, His faithfulness heals us.

This healing is a process. God works in our lives, faithfully molding us bit by bit into the character-likeness of Christ Jesus. The Holy Spirit heals our memories gradually, one relationship or one experience at a time. He deals with us regarding our sins, but again it's one at a time. He addresses our bad habits and our lack of knowledge or understanding, and He does it one issue at a time.

For our healing to continue, we must join the process by carrying out certain things faithfully and consistently. In our physical lives, one day of exercise is not the same as 30 minutes of exercise several times a week. The same is true for our spiritual lives. Reading the Bible for an hour once a month isn't as beneficial as reading the Bible ten minutes a day for a month. Praying only when we have a pressing need isn't as beneficial as setting aside time daily to praise, thank, petition, and worship God. It's what we do faithfully that produces wholeness.

If you have been forsaken by a friend, you understand the pain of betrayal. But God can never betray you. The closer you draw to Him, the more you will experience the wholeness and healing that come from trusting in His faithfulness.

This you can count on...not because I say it, but because you have God's Word.

Who is like you, LORD God Almighty?
You, LORD, are mighty, and your
faithfulness surrounds you...
Righteousness and justice are the foundation of your throne;
love and faithfulness go before you.

PSALM 89:8, 14

Dear God, I praise You and thank You for being true to Your Word and to the words You speak to my heart. I recommit to placing my trust in Your faithfulness, which I experience in many ways. Just as You were there for Your disciples whenever they faced troubles, You are here for me. You are faithful in Your forgiveness and in Your love. You provided the Holy Spirit to continue leading so that no believer is left an orphan but is given comfort and guidance. I'm grateful because I couldn't do this life without Him. And I know I would not be able to be a person of honor without the conviction of the Spirit.

Lord, help me demonstrate my trust in You and become faithful in the ways I am called to be obedient, disciplined, and committed, whether with small things or big things. Amen.

39

COURAGE TO BE MEEK

Life has many burdens. Have you felt the weight of them lately? Responsibilities, tasks, efforts, and connections often zap the energy out of us. When someone offers to take even one thing off your plate, it can be a great relief…that is, if you will let him.

As believers, we have a God who is asking to be our strength, our help. Yet if you are like me, you have held on to a few burdens out of stubbornness or a skewed sense of independence. It's easy to buy into the belief that life and achievements are only valued when we have created them in our power. It's harder to believe God has our back when we release the control.

Until we trust God, our striving puts us into ongoing competition with other people because in seeking to raise ourselves up, we inevitably put others down. We see every other person as a rival. You may not think you have a "me vs. them" mindset, but when you continue to do everything without partnering with the Lord and others, you have set up that dynamic.

Some Bible versions translate the spiritual fruit of gentleness as "meekness." This meekness produces healing and wholeness in us by removing the great stress and weight of self-defense and self-promotion. In their place, meekness brings freedom. Freedom to rest in the Lord's strength.

You might be wondering, *Who wants to be called meek?* The common interpretation is that meekness means weakness or timidity. Yet nothing could be further from the truth. The Greek word for "meekness," *praotes*, is synonymous with courage, confidence, security, and strength under control. The phrase "gentle giant" is similar in meaning to the concept of *praotes*. A gentle giant is big, strong, and capable of destruction. However, the gentleness of this person causes him to care for the weak, defend the helpless, and nurture the innocent. A gentle giant is strong in character and resolve, yet tender and humble before God.

In the Bible, Moses is described as the meekest man on the face of the earth. In some translations he is called humble. If you have studied the life of Moses, you know already that he was anything but weak or cowardly. Moses was a strong and decisive leader, and he was completely yielded to God.

The truly meek person stands in humility before God, knowing that all he has, all he does, and all he is, he owes to God. God gives him every heartbeat, every good and productive idea, every opportunity. The meek person knows that because of God, she has all things, can do all things, and will accomplish all that God commands her to do, even when it feels daunting. This person of gentle spirit and submission rightly claims that all abilities and success come from God and lays all accolades at the feet of Jesus to say, "You alone are worthy."

When we grow this fruit of the Spirit, we recognize that we are nothing without God. And in that knowing, we are given great strength and reward. In the Sermon on the Mount, Jesus says, "Blessed are the meek, for they will inherit the earth" (Matthew 5:5).

Reap the healing of meekness in your life. When you recognize that God is in charge, you will experience richer relationships because you will have traded competition for collaboration. You will know emotional, physical, and spiritual health as you lay your burdens down. That is the healing work of God's gentle but powerful meekness in your life.

Do you trust God enough to humble yourself before Him? Can you let go of the idea that you were ever meant to do life or find success alone? Come to

God with the courage to be meek, and you will be strengthened by His Spirit. His best for You is waiting to be expressed through your humility.

Humility is the fear of the LORD;
   its wages are riches and honor and life.

PROVERBS 22:4

God, I want to experience the wholeness that comes through the fruit of meekness. I want to give honor and glory to Your name, not mine, because there is power in Your name, not mine. When I start to build up myself, remind me of this and that my value is in You alone. Keep me from viewing others as competition. That never serves Your purposes. Like Moses, I want to obey You with the courage to follow where You lead and to inspire others to know Your voice and ways.

In a culture where self-preservation rules, empower me, Lord, to look out for other people. I want to be strong, kind, and humble because I know I am nothing without You. This world needs the healing that comes with the strength and tenderness of the meek. Help me to be one of them. Amen.

40

THE MYSTERIOUS HEALING
OF SELF-CONTROL

D o you love a good mystery? Our journey of healing with the Lord presents us with many of them. One could say the ways of God are not always intuitive for the human heart and mind to grasp.

One of those great mysteries is the way the Holy Spirit works in us: To be self-disciplined, we must yield control of self. Who wants to give up control? The fact is, we all routinely yield control of our lives to forces outside ourselves. We yield to the law of gravity when we trip and fall. We yield the right of way to other motorists to avoid an accident. We yield to the wishes of our supervisors at work to get our jobs done.

The Holy Spirit calls us to be like Jesus in living a God-ordered life and in remaining totally committed to doing things God's way. We must invite the Holy Spirit to daily fill up our lives. Otherwise, we will be filled with the impulses of the world, the flesh, and the devil. The Spirit calls us to maintain a passion for excellence in serving God and others. And the Holy Spirit supplies all the power we need to live a disciplined, God-honoring life.

Contrary to the world's beliefs, the spiritual fruit of self-control does not come about through the discipline of self-mastery, but rather through surrendering ourselves to God's control. The self-control of the Holy Spirit is a character trait, not just a daily discipline. It shows up in our lives in different ways. Maybe it's hearing God say to us, "Speak to that person now" and then going ahead to speak, without asking, "But how will she respond?" Or hearing God say, "Go to a certain place, and when you get there, do this," and then doing what He commands without making any excuses. It's the ultimate obedience and, mysteriously, the ultimate freedom.

The spiritual fruit of self-control heals us, in large measure, by bringing order to the chaos of life. When we recognize that God has created us, called us, and equipped us to undertake a specific mission, much of our life comes into focus. We know who we are and what we are to accomplish. We know that the foremost goal God has for us is that we follow Jesus as our Lord.

As we seek to do His will and not our own, we are free to take risks, speak boldly, and face life honestly. When we faithfully trust God, we can know He will take everything we do with a sincere heart and turn it into something good within the context of His greater plan and purpose.

When we yield our lives to the daily filling of the Holy Spirit, we give Him an opportunity to show us what needs to be removed from our lives and what needs to be added. He helps us craft our schedules and new sets of habits, dreams, goals, and plans—all of which combine to produce the person He desires us to become. The more we align ourselves with His commands and His plan, the more we lead a focused, disciplined, and purposeful life. And in this lifelong process, we become whole.

As the Holy Spirit heals you, certainly you will be blessed. But the greater benefit goes to those who receive your embrace of compassion and words of encouragement. Your wisdom and integrity will serve them. As you bear the fruit of the Holy Spirit, you will extend the blessing of God to those around you.

Place yourself under the guidance of God's Spirit today. He is more than equal to the challenge of healing your brokenness and putting the pieces of your life into an order that not only makes sense, but also makes beautiful the offering of your life. This is true spiritual healing.

The grace of God has appeared that offers salvation to all people. It teaches us to say "No" to ungodliness and worldly passions, and to live self-controlled, upright and godly lives in this present age, while we wait for the blessed hope—the appearing of the glory of our great God and Savior, Jesus Christ.

Titus 2:11-13

Dear Lord, I admit I struggle with surrender, but I long to place my life under Your control. What good are my efforts if they don't result in living out the purpose You shape for me? These goals of mine are merely dust if they are only of my making.

Today, I lift my life to Your capable hands and compassionate heart. I am excited to discover how You will lead me with the fruit of self-control. Reveal Your plan for me and bless me with all I need to live it out. I have been getting by...even finding success here and there, but neither my efforts nor the world's offerings bring contentment. My deepest spiritual healing comes only through You and the fruit of the Spirit. I place my hope in Your grace and praise You for the amazing peace that rises from a surrendered heart. Amen.

PRAISING HIM AS MY REFUGE, MY STRENGTH

Enter his gates with thanksgiving
and his courts with praise.
Give thanks to him and praise his name.

PSALM 100:4

My soul will rejoice in the LORD;
it shall delight in his salvation.
My whole being will exclaim,
"Who is like you, LORD?"

PSALM 35:9-10

Praise the Lord!

If King David were with us today, I have no doubt he would sound a clarion call to every believer using those very words: Praise the Lord! He would call us to clap our hands, to make a joyful noise to almighty God with musical instruments, and to shout praises to the Most High! He would be animated. He would implore us to join him as he praises our Lord with song and dance and even times of lying face-down on the ground confessing to God His greatness.

To our Western way of thinking, this might seem a bit overbearing. But let me help you see things from David's perspective. I am by birth and by upbringing a Middle Easterner, so I understand this man's passion. In the Middle East, you don't greet a friend with a casual hello. Even if you have just seen that friend the day before, you greet him warmly when you see him again. Often, you will embrace him. Encountering a friend is a cause for gladness.

How much more, then, would a Middle Easterner such as David express his feelings when encountering the Lord Most High, the God who loves us far more than any friend ever could? You can understand why, if David were here today, he would insist that we put our whole hearts into our praise of God. Would you gladly heed his call to praise God with your entire being—all that you are, all that you have, and all that you will ever be—every day of your life?

In this last third of our devotional journey together, your eyes will be opened to the wonder of the God we praise, and more than ever you will understand why He deserves unfailing glory and honor…the exact praise, my friend, that you can offer.

41

THE PURPOSE OF PRAISE

Let's praise the Lord!" Okay, maybe you aren't hearing King David express this invitation, but chances are you hear it in church or in conversations with other believers. What matters is how you respond whenever you hear it. Does it inspire words of gratitude and awe to flow? Or do you hesitate because it feels like a request for an obligatory shout-out to God? I regularly encounter Christians who respond with something in the middle. They are honest in their appreciation of God, yet they view praise as something we do only for God.

When the great scholar and writer C.S. Lewis became a new believer, he was troubled by the Bible's commands to praise God. He saw it as a dry exchange God was requiring. We tell Him how great He is, and then God does something for us.

The truth is far more healing, my friend. Praise is not a program by which we manipulate God to answer our prayer requests. No! Praise flows naturally from our relationship of love and devotion to the Lord. The purpose of praise is to honor God, draw close to Him, and prepare our hearts to receive benefits and blessings from Him. As we become faithful in our acts of worship, our relationship with the Lord grows deeper, richer, and more personal.

As Lewis grew in his faith, he discovered the importance of a daily surrender to the lordship of Jesus Christ. He had a complete perspective shift: "Only in the act of worship and praise can a person learn to believe in the goodness and the greatness of God. God wants us to praise him, not because he needs or craves, in any sense, our flattery. But because he knows that praise creates joy and thankfulness."*

There are simple ways to make praise a part of your fellowship with God. When you talk to Him, include praise to start or close your prayer. Read the psalms aloud when you rise or before you go to bed. Find times to turn up the praise music, and let it carry your spirit to God's presence. Soon you will discover the heart changes of praise that lead us to love God and others with zeal. You will experience spiritual growth and development. And you will be participating in the great engine that drives the church forward, resulting in deeper faith, a more powerful witness, and amazing victories in the spiritual realm. When the body of Christ praises the Lord, joy and gratitude reign.

Praise is more than an obligation, more than a simple spiritual exercise. It's the path that brings us near to God and to His love, power, and grace. It ushers us to a more intimate relationship with our Creator and Savior, and to a more fulfilling life on this earth.

Every person I know, in the depths of his or her heart, seeks a life of fulfillment and joy. We are driven to know our reason for being. We want our lives to make a difference, to bring out something of lasting value. As the saying goes, we don't want much—we want everything, at least everything that matters. God is *that* everything.

To find meaning for our life, we need to concentrate on praising Him. As we are brought into closer communion with God, He reveals things to us about ourselves. Praise opens our eyes to spiritual reality, to the love and power of God, and to our desperate need for Him.

Praise is the ultimate empowering adventure. In praising God, we have a

---

* Adapted from C.S. Lewis, *Reflections on the Psalms* (San Diego: Harvest Book/Harcourt, 1986), 93-95.

chance to really know who we are, and we'll begin to experience the great mystery and power of God's work. This is the greatest exhilaration a person can know.

Praise the LORD, my soul,
 and forget not all his benefits—
who forgives all your sins
 and heals all your diseases,
who redeems your life from the pit
 and crowns you with love and compassion,
who satisfies your desires with good things
 so that your youth is renewed like the eagle's.

PSALM 103:2-5

Bring on the joy, Lord. Forgive me for the times I neglect to make praise a vital part of my prayers and our relationship. My first thoughts are often of my need for help, provision, and solutions. It's one of the pitfalls of being in a culture that leans toward "what's in it for me" more than "who can I praise for the opportunity of this life?" I don't want to be a fair-weather person of praise. I want to honor Your goodness, forgiveness, mercy, and redemptive love whether it is stormy or sunny.

Praising You, in turn, fills me with hope and joy. I'm at Your feet looking up, and this perspective reminds me I'm not the one in control but beloved by the One who is. Gratitude flows from this realization. I give to You my devotion, God. You are worthy and wonderful. Amen.

42

PRAISE IS PERSONAL

S top for a moment to consider this truth: Nobody can praise God exactly the way you do because no one else has had your exact experiences. No one has known God's presence and power in the same way you have. You and God have your own history and journey together. The experiences you draw from to honor God are yours alone. Your praise is a unique expression, reflecting your relationship with the Lord. It fulfills part of your distinctive destiny as a uniquely created human being with one life to live.

And what is the purpose of that life? If we were to ask Paul that question, he would surely say again what he declares of God in Scripture: "In love he predestined us for adoption to sonship through Jesus Christ, in accordance with his pleasure and will—to the praise of his glorious grace" (Ephesians 1:4-6).

If we were to ask Isaiah, he might remind us that God spoke of His people as "the people I formed for myself that they may proclaim my praise" (Isaiah 43:21).

If we were to ask Peter, he might proclaim again that even the purpose of our suffering and trials is that our faith "may result in praise, glory and honor when Jesus Christ is revealed" (1 Peter 1:7).

And what if we asked Jesus? He might recall for us that day when He entered Jerusalem while a great crowd shouted joyful praises to God: "When he came near the place where the road goes down the Mount of Olives, the whole crowd of disciples began joyfully to praise God in loud voices for all the miracles they had seen: 'Blessed is the king who comes in the name of the Lord!' 'Peace in heaven and glory in the highest!'" (Luke 19:37-38).

Now think about your response. If your purpose is to praise the Lord, what informs and shapes your praise? Your first thoughts may be of the blessings you have received from God's provision. Or think back to the point you encountered God as your personal Lord for the first time. Praise Him for changing your life when you became an adopted child through Jesus Christ.

While we don't always think to praise God for our adversity, the trials and challenges we face are often exactly what we need to draw us close to His heart. When we feel unsure of which way to go, we may go running to the Lord's presence with a trust and urgency we might not have on the smooth sailing days.

Have you had a season of discouragement or heartbreak that led you to the foot of the cross? Or a particular moment when you realized you were walking away from God, and His grace covered you and redirected you to His embrace and His path for you?

Your praise is extremely personal. While you may draw from the praises of the faithful in the Bible, take time to also weave in your many reasons to praise the Lord. Your heart becomes tethered to His when you shift to praying and praising based on your unique journey, relationship, love, and experience with the Almighty. Consider what has transpired in just the past few days and weeks that inspires you to praise God. When you hold your salvation as a gift of sacrifice from God, what words of thanksgiving and awe come to mind and tumble from your heart?

When the Pharisees admonished Jesus that He should rebuke people for praising Him, Jesus replied, "I tell you...if they keep quiet, the stones will cry out" (Luke 19:40). Creation's purpose is to enjoy fellowship with God that results in praise to Him, and if God's people fail to fulfill this purpose, the inanimate rocks will shout praises in their place.

I don't know about you, but I certainly don't want a rock doing my job!

LORD, you alone are my portion and my cup;
   you make my lot secure.
The boundary lines have fallen for me in pleasant places;
   surely I have a delightful inheritance.

PSALM 16:5-6

Praise You, Lord! I look back at all I have been through with You as my Companion, Guide, Provider, and Savior, and my heart is full. My journey has included mountains to climb and valleys to endure that tested my faith and patience, and through it all You were there. You are Creator of all I hold with gratitude—from the beauty of nature to the laughter of my friends to the difficulties that make me get on my knees with a humble spirit.

I'm thankful that Scripture provides many examples of reasons to praise Your holy name. I witness how troubles or joys inspire the praises of Your children. I am a part of that history, Lord. Every day I can respond to my personal difficulties and triumphs with a heart of gratitude for Your presence. That is yet another reason to praise You. Amen.

43

ALL OF YOU

A man stood in a midweek prayer meeting and began to pray, "O Lord, I will praise You with the instrument of ten strings." Just about everybody in the room opened at least one eye because we knew no musical instruments were around. I could sense a feeling of bewilderment throughout the prayer group. How was this man going to praise the Lord with a ten-stringed instrument?

He continued his prayer:

> I will praise You with my two eyes. I will look only to You. I will praise You by exalting You with my two ears—I will listen only to Your voice. I will extol You with the work of my two hands. I will work in Your service wherever You direct. I will honor You with my two feet. I will walk in Your statutes, and I will go wherever You lead. I will magnify Your holy name with my tongue. I will testify constantly to Your loving-kindness. I will worship You with my heart—I will love only You, and I will receive all the unconditional love You pour out in Your mercy, grace, and forgiveness. I thank You, Lord, for the ten-stringed instrument You built into my being. Keep me in tune and play upon me as You will. Ring out the melodies of Your grace. May the harmony of my praise song bring pleasure to You and glory to Your name. Amen.

This man knew about praising God with everything that was within him. We are to praise the Lord with our minds, offer praise from our hearts, and voice praise with our mouths.

Let's follow his lead and praise God with our full selves. Turning to Scripture, we can become an instrument of praise to honor God and to commit every part of us to worship.

With our mouths: "With my mouth I will greatly extol the LORD; in the great throng of worshipers I will praise him" (Psalm 109:30).

With our hands: "Lift up your hands in the sanctuary and praise the LORD" (Psalm 134:2).

With our ears: "Let me hear joy and gladness" (Psalm 51:8).

With our eyes: "My heart says of you, 'Seek his face!' Your face, LORD, I will seek" (Psalm 27:8).

With our hearts: "I will praise you, Lord my God, with all my heart; I will glorify your name forever" (Psalm 86:12).

Soon the whole of our personal life becomes a living act of praise. Think about the power and beauty of living each day with full awareness that you are praising God in your conversations, interactions, decisions, the work of your hands and mind, and the priorities you set. Even if you are not saying "Praise the Lord" each time you see your mail carrier or dentist, the way you engage with that person and express the love of God *is* its own version of praise.

When all of you points to all of Him, you are embracing a full life of praise and are bringing Him glory. How might your ways and days change? Consider how you will approach God's throne as a ten-stringed instrument ready to sing and play your praises to His goodness and eternal love.

Give praise to the Lord, proclaim his name;
    make known among the nations what he has done.
Sing to him, sing praise to him;
    tell of all his wonderful acts.
Glory in his holy name;
    let the hearts of those who seek the Lord rejoice.

1 Chronicles 16:8-10

Lord my God, my deepest desire is to praise You and to love You with all my heart, all my soul, all my mind, and all my strength. I can express that praise to You daily through the words that come from my mouth and the ways I engage with people You bring to my path. God, let me begin by praising You in front of my family as I strive to serve them with a heart of ministry and unconditional love. May they see the difference in me. May they see You in me.

I feel my heart shift in my chest as I look at my life with fresh eyes and a mind and spirit of praise. When I rise and thank You for a new day, may I anticipate with gladness how I can surrender every part of me to point others to all of You. Amen.

44

EMPOWERED BY PRAISE

I grew up in Egypt under the influence of a Christian family. I often sang songs of praise to God, and I would hear my mother and my grandfather praise God for hours at a time. But though I became a believer in Jesus Christ as a young man, I didn't begin to grasp the true meaning of praise until the spring of 1990.

That's when my lovely wife, Elizabeth, was diagnosed with cancer. She was barely 40 years old.

My first thought was, *Lord, she's too young to have breast cancer! How can this be happening?* My emotional protest was a way of dealing with my fear. I had trouble praying without being overwhelmed with worry over what might happen. I had trouble sleeping, lying awake in bed with a troubled heart. But amid the terrible fear that I might lose my beloved wife, and the frustration that I could not take her place or do anything to protect her except to pray for her, I began to truly learn the power of praise.

Our church was only three years old at the time, and our congregation was still small. But we immediately committed ourselves to intercession. We entered God's course of instruction, "Power of Praise 101," with the Holy Spirit and the Bible as our instructors. God began to take me, my family, and our church through the first stages of learning what it means to praise Him while standing in the full force of the storm. The more we praised God, the stronger our belief grew that He is capable of all things. His heart breaks with the very same things that force us to our knees. And He is infinitely compassionate toward His hurting and needy children.

We learned a lasting lesson during the time that my wife was battling cancer. The more we praised God, even while in the desert of unknowing, the deeper the fellowship we experienced with Him. As my wife underwent medical treatment that slowly brought physical healing, we underwent spiritual treatment that brought wholeness, hope, strength, and power to our souls.

Our spiritual wholeness, and our experience of God's power, came about through praising Him. Our fear over my wife's illness gave way to greater faith in God's rule over our circumstances. Praise fully established the reign of God in our lives.

What worries or fears interrupt your prayers and praises? It isn't wrong to have them...just don't let them stop the flow of your conversation with God. Turn them into an offering and make them a part of your prayer and praise. As we celebrated in the previous devotion, bringing all of yourself into your praise honors God and fills Him with delight. Giving over your anxieties and concerns to His hands is a way to bring ALL you carry to Him.

Ultimately, praise reinforces the truth of who we are and who God is. He alone is the One who makes us whole. He alone is the One who walks through the dark valley with us. Our faithful Lord never leaves us nor forsakes us. He alone is the Source of all good things.

Praise the Lord! My wife made it through that journey. We continue to praise God not only for her healing but also for teaching us what it means to be empowered by praise to face any terror, any threat, and any problem life may hand us. Now I am grateful I grew up with praise and later learned to grow into praise as a way of living.

Allow yourself the amazing opportunity to seek the Source of all good things and to drink in all of Him no matter what you face. You will be strengthened, and you will discover how joy exists even in a difficult season. Imagine yourself in the embrace of God.

⌒

To him who is able to do immeasurably more than all we ask or imagine, according to his power that is at work within us, to him be glory in the church and in Christ Jesus throughout all generations, for ever and ever! Amen.

EPHESIANS 3:20-21

I praise You for Your power, almighty God. What a giving God You are that You allow me to come to You in every circumstance. I can be in Your presence broken and troubled, and Your tender mercy and love cover me. Why then should I ever give power to fear instead of faith? I know who You are. From Scripture and personal experience, I trust Your character and Your promises. Because of Your faithfulness, I view my trials as opportunities to draw close to You and depend on Your power.

You do immeasurably more than I can imagine, according to Your will and purpose. Your answer to my prayer might be different from what I want in my limited wisdom. Still, I trust in You. Whether I wander my desert of unknowing or I walk a clear path set before me, I will praise You. Amen.

$$\left(45\right)$$

BUILDING ON BELIEF

The Scriptures tell us that our lips reveal whatever we treasure in our hearts. Jesus said, "The mouth speaks what the heart is full of" (Matthew 12:34). Ultimately, we cannot separate what we say and do from what we think and believe deep inside.

If we truly believe in God's love and goodness, that belief will spill over into what we say about Him. No matter what our circumstances are, we won't be able to hold back our praise. Do we truly believe God is the almighty King of the universe and the Lord of our lives? The strength and fervor, the depth and energy of our praise to God—both with our lips and in our lives—is directly proportional to our belief in God's goodness and greatness.

Belief and praise build on each other. The more deeply and strongly we believe, the greater and more expansive is our praise. The more we praise the Lord, the more we will behold His glory and see His hand continually at work in our lives, and the more fervently and strongly we will believe.

Never is this truth tested more than when a loved one is in danger, such as when my wife's cancer was diagnosed. Another person very close to me was gravely ill at the same time. To see two people I loved facing the unknown, possibly even the threat of death itself, tested my beliefs about God. Was He really a God of love, of healing, and of faithfulness? Or was He unconcerned about my family's health and safety?

For most of my life, I had believed the former: That God, in His faithfulness, loves us and cares for us and brings healing. So from this foundation of belief, I praised Him in advance for His care, His comfort, and His power to heal. In praising Him, I wholeheartedly believed that God is who He says He is. The certainty of His shelter and provision during that time remains with me to this day.

Before I knew the outcomes for my loved ones' health, I knew without question that God loves us without limit and that He heals us by His power. My life changed from the obedience of duty to the joyful, visceral obedience that expresses itself in uninhibited praise to our loving and all-powerful Lord.

What are your beliefs about God that help build your ability to praise Him? We explored in earlier devotions how praise is personal. Look back at a time when God's faithfulness provided solid ground for your shaky first steps toward a new beginning. Did His conviction of your spirit save you from something that could have cost you integrity or relationship? Has God ever met you in the middle of the night with a rush of love and grace that washed away anxiety? How has His presence been your stability and your comfort when a hard season remained difficult?

We have so many reasons to praise Him, friend. If this is a new way of experiencing God and your faith, consider keeping a list with examples of God's presence. With each one, there is another stone in the foundation of your belief in who He is and what relationship with Him accomplishes, not only in your life but as He influences others through His work in you. You will gain a new way of seeing and living. You will notice God's faithfulness as it happens and be present to His presence. And your lips will be ready to praise because your belief has prepared your mind and heart to honor Him.

God really is the loving Father who comforts us in our times of deepest desperation, fear, and helplessness. That is a truth we can believe, build on, and praise Him for.

⌒

Very truly I tell you, whoever believes in me will do the works I have been doing, and they will do even greater things than these, because I am going to the Father. And I will do whatever you ask in my name, so that the Father may be glorified in the Son.

JOHN 14:12-13

My Savior Jesus, I believe because You have helped me to overcome my unbelief. You have filled my heart to overflowing by pouring into my life love, grace, healing, kindness, and mercy. My foundation of belief is rising as each day there are new examples of Your faithfulness. I stand on that belief and raise my hands to praise You. Though my memories of Your care are plentiful and empowering, I don't need to look far back for evidence of Your love for me because now I am in the habit of seeing it every day.

I praise You, Father. Thank You for all the times You have guided me away from destructive paths or calmed my spirit when I or people I love have faced trials. I open my life to Your work so that You can work through me in Jesus's name. Amen.

OUR FREEWILL OFFERING

The world causes hassles for us every day. Our fears, anxieties, and hurts are very real. But if we focus only on these earthly problems, then soon the spiritual realm becomes foggy and unreal. We can lose sight of God and slide into pessimism and even depression. Life loses its joy and excitement. If we limit our thinking to this world alone, it will grind us down into the dust from which we were created.

No matter how difficult or unjust our circumstances become, we can exercise our free will and choose to praise God rather than ignore Him. We can choose not only what we will praise Him for, but how long, how frequently, and how intensely we will praise Him.

We don't often think of practicing our free will in terms of how we have fellowship with God. Usually that phrase comes up when we are talking about our choice of being saved by Christ and placed under His forgiveness and eternal grace. How might this perspective of praise as a freewill offering change the way you approach your times of prayer? Every day you have a choice in how you serve and honor the Lord.

When are you inspired to choose to glorify God?

If you've ever experienced a powerfully moving praise service at church, you know firsthand that though praise has a strong emotional dimension, it's not driven by emotions. Praise is driven by our will. That's why we must never say, "I prefer to wait and praise God when I really feel like it." We're to praise God in all situations, in both victory and defeat, when we're in need and when we're experiencing plenty.

In fact, the times when you don't feel like praising God are precisely the moments when it's most essential to do so. The next time you are discouraged, start praising God. When you feel defeated or unable to break loose from bad habits, start praising God. When your most treasured relationships seem to be falling apart, start praising God.

Why do I say this? Because praise is about what God desires us to do. It's not about the power of your circumstances. When you take your eyes off your immediate problem and put your focus on God, you redirect yourself toward what He will do for you, not what man has done to you. At that point, God can work in your life to produce real growth.

Have you ever tried this in the past? How did it go? Did you have a change of perspective and heart? It can take practice to develop the spiritual muscle of going to God for all things. We get caught up in our lives and the individual moments that make them up. God wants you to include Him in all of those moments. The highs and lows. The uncertainties and the celebrations. The times of grief and times of gladness.

The truth for the believer is that this tangible, physical world is not the "real" world. The real world is our ultimate home—the heavenly, spiritual realm where God's presence permeates the atmosphere. When we start to view our present life in light of this ultimate reality, things begin to change. Faith and hope take root and flourish; joy and peace grow in our hearts. What starts as a change in perspective transforms into a fuel, a desire to be in the Lord's presence while we are here on Earth and in anticipation of the eternity we will spend with Him. Don't you want to know everything you can about the One you will spend forever with?

Praise focuses our attention on the world of the Spirit—the heavenly, spiritual reality where He calls us to live. Experience the transformation of your disposition, feelings, perspective, and heart when you praise God even in hard times. Lift up your freewill offering of praise today.

I will sacrifice a freewill offering to you;
　　I will praise your name, Lord, for it is good.

Psalm 54:6

Lord, I'm sorry for the times I have held back my praise and treated it as an exchange, waiting for just the right blessing to happen or for the right feeling to come over me. Thanks to Your grace and sacrifice, my praise is a freewill offering. You are not an arrogant king demanding compliments. You are the mighty King of kings who is worthy of my praise no matter what.

Without conditions I will lift praises because You are You. As I walk forward in faith and with gratitude, I won't wait for my situation to be perfect or my mood to be light before I exalt You and praise Your name. I turn my eyes from my circumstances, and I look to You full of love. It is my honor to serve and praise You for the rest of my life on earth and for eternity. Amen.

47

GOD DWELLS IN YOUR PRAISE

An amazing thing happens as we praise God for all He is and does. We clearly see the truth of His nature. We understand that He is the unlimited, holy, eternal King. We recognize that He is all-knowing, all-wise, and all-powerful. We experience Him as loving, merciful, and long-suffering.

When we come to God in praise and adoration, we also see more clearly the truth about ourselves, including the truth of our sinfulness and unworthiness. Let me openly confess that I have never come into the presence of God—praising Him, adoring Him, and honoring Him with the fruit of my lips—when I did not also become more conscious of my own limitations, faults, and sins.

The more we grasp all that God is, the more we face all that we are not. Job was a man so godly that God bragged about him, but when God revealed His great power, Job replied in humility, "I know that you can do all things; no plan of yours can be thwarted" (Job 42:2). "My ears had heard of you but now my eyes have seen you. Therefore I despise myself and repent in dust and ashes" (Job 42:5-6).

No matter how righteous we are, seeing God's glory confronts us with the tarnish and stain of our own lives. The reason for this is not to make us walk through life with our heads hanging low but that we might repent of our sin and rely on God and cry out to Him to forgive us and to strengthen us by the power of His Holy Spirit. Instead of being downcast about our failings and weakness, we can celebrate our strength in Him. We can go about our days awestruck and inspired because our praise leads us to His power and presence.

In fact, the Scriptures tell us that God dwells in the praises of His people. He is the holy God "that inhabitest the praises of Israel" (Psalm 22:3 KJV). The image painted by the psalmist is that God sits down and takes delight in the praises offered to His name. God pitches His tent wherever His name is exalted. He camps out with those who acknowledge and glorify Him and desire to be with Him. Through praise we experience more fully God's presence, both within us and at work all around us.

If you're struggling with pain, sickness, or loss and are desperate for a sense of God's nearness, then start praising His holy name. As my wife and I recoiled at the surgeon's word "cancer," we clung to God in praise of His love, His protection, and His faithfulness. We needed Him to set up camp amid our weakness and fear and suffering. And He did!

The simple fact of God's presence is this: Wherever God dwells, God rules. He is our authority. When we invite God to dwell in us, He reigns over our hearts. When we invite God to dwell in our marriages and our family relationships, He reigns over those relationships. When we invite God to extend His will and presence in our business, He reigns over our business.

Praise is our foremost means of inviting God to take up His residence with us and to establish His presence, authority, and purpose in every area of our lives. As we praise our Lord, we enjoy the warmest, deepest form of fellowship with our heavenly Father.

Praise God because He gives us an opportunity to see our sin so we can ask Him to work in us and change us into the men and women we truly desire to become. The prayer of our hearts should always be "God, make me into the person You want to live with forever!"

No matter what you are facing, praise Him now. Enter each day knowing you are blessed with the opportunity to welcome the Lord to inhabit your prayers, praises, and life.

I will praise the LORD, who counsels me;
    even at night my heart instructs me.
I keep my eyes always on the LORD.
    With him at my right hand, I will not be shaken.
Therefore my heart is glad and my tongue rejoices;
    my body also will rest secure.

PSALM 16:7-9

Lord, thank You for coming to dwell within me and for making my heart Your home. Because You have done this, I am "filled with an inexpressible and glorious joy" like never before. Anything I aspire to is a shadow of what and who You are. Rejoicing in Your greatness magnifies my limits and humbles me. This also ushers me right back to Your presence where I want front row seats to witness Your wonder and love.

Who do You want me to become in my time on Earth and in eternity, Lord? Counsel me and instruct my heart even as I sleep. I want less of me and more of You with each passing day, Lord. It brings me comfort to know that in my weakness, You are strong. In my frailty, You are invincible. I pray my praise is where You will always dwell. Amen.

48

DEVOTION TO GOD

When I was a boy growing up in Egypt, my grandfather was a building contractor by trade and a lay leader in the Brethren Church. He lived in a small apartment adjacent to the home of my cousins, and when I spent the night with them, I'd find myself waking up several times during the night. From his apartment next door, I would hear my grandfather praising the Lord. He seemed to praise God around the clock.

My grandfather lost two sons when they were in their early thirties, and he lost his wife while he was still a relatively young man, but he was always full of joy. Praise gave my grandfather his joyful heart. Until he died at the age of 92, he never ceased to praise God throughout the night and then again in the morning.

My mother had grown up with this man's model of devotion to God, and it shaped her life. It wasn't unusual for her to pray for one or two hours at a time. She had developed this spiritual discipline of prayer and praise from observing her father. Nothing the world offers could ever compare with this rich spiritual legacy I inherited from my mother and grandfather.

Why should we praise God? Perhaps the foremost reason is the one evident in the life of my grandfather: joy. We praise God as an expression of our joy in Him, and that praise in turn produces in us a life of deep and abiding joy.

If you are discouraged and joy seems distant, I want to encourage you. To those who know this exhaustion, God offers a hope that energizes us. The prophet Isaiah told us that those who hope in the Lord have their strength renewed and their energy restored (see Isaiah 40:31). But how do we acquire this hope?

We become hopeful when we look at what God can do, not at what man has done or attempts to do. And what else happens when we turn our attention to all that God can do? Our spirit desires to praise Him for who He is. The response of our heart is to reach beyond our human fatigue or frailty and thank God for the hope of His strength and renewal.

In turn, more hope springs up as we praise God for His perfection and as we recognize, acknowledge, and trust in all that He is, rather than giving honor to—or being discouraged by—our imperfections. If you're exhausted at the end of the day, spend alone time with God. Praise Him with every ounce of energy that remains in you. You'll be refreshed not only mentally and emotionally but also physically. There's a special strength that is imparted to those who praise the Lord. This kind of strength gives you the power of hope to endure, to persevere, to outlast tough times. It gives you the power to intercede until God provides a breakthrough.

I am 100 percent convinced that the best medicine for spiritual exhaustion is praise. Praise fuels joy, a joy like no other. Isn't it incredible that our devotion to God stirs within us greater joy and hope than we could ever know otherwise? Even as God is honored, He finds ways to bless us.

You can't read the book of Revelation without realizing that the joy of praise forms the atmosphere of heaven. What an unspeakably glorious praise song is filling heaven this very minute. I have no doubt that my grandfather and mother are part of that great praise choir! What joy to know that we who are in Christ Jesus will be praising God and adoring Him forever. Our bodies may be buried on this earth, but our praise will never die. It will go on forever.

Even youths grow tired and weary,
    and young men stumble and fall;
but those who hope in the LORD
    will renew their strength.
They will soar on wings like eagles;
    they will run and not grow weary,
they will walk and not be faint.

ISAIAH 40:30-31

Lord, when I lift up Your name and praise You, You bless me with renewed joy. In seasons of exhaustion, it's my focus on You that restores my hope and confidence in all that You are capable of doing in my circumstances and in my heart. Your strength infuses me, carries me, and challenges me to move forward in faith and conviction. I am energized by Your love. Before I know it, my praises become stronger and louder. They rise from a spirit that is encouraged by Your love and nature. You, in turn, bless me further. Such love You show me, Lord.

As my soul's devotion is made evident in my praise, may it give You joy. The words of honor and gratitude I lift to You today are just my earthly warm-up for the songs I will sing in the praise choir in heaven. Amen.

OPEN TO GOD

Have you ever noticed how your view of God determines your praise, and thus your praise mirrors your view of God?

The word "worship" comes from "worth-ship," which means expressing to God His worth to us. How much do you value who God is? How much do you value what God has done for you? How much do you rely daily on what God promises to do for you? How much worth do you place on your relationship with Him? What is your view of Him?

If you believe He is your loving, patient, and forgiving heavenly Father, your praise will reflect those qualities of God.

If you believe He cares about you every moment and in every circumstance, then you're likely to be praising God all the time! "Praise the Lord" will be something you say in one form or another countless times throughout the day.

If you're deeply grateful that God has saved you from the consequences of your sin, you'll have so much praise that you cannot express it all in just a few moments. Your praise will be overflowing and ongoing because your gratitude is so great.

If you see God as fully willing to move heaven and Earth on your behalf, your praise will be enthusiastic and heartfelt! Those who see Him as being on their side, working always for their eternal benefit, are those who praise Him with the most intensity and the greatest amount of faith.

Praise brings us to a fuller recognition of God—not so that we might cower before Him, but so that we might bow before Him in humble worship. We worship God not so much to do something for Him, although He does desire our praise, but we worship Him to affirm His lordship and to submit our lives to His lordship. When you open your life to your heavenly Father with a heart of praise, your priorities align with His purposes.

In fact, that truth helps explain why praise can be difficult for us. Praise demands that we make changes in our lives, and most of us don't welcome the prospect of change. It takes courage to reexamine what we believe to be true about ourselves and about God and to realize what we need to change about our lives.

Sometimes the change God commands will require us to confess and repent of a sin and to adjust how we live, especially how we think of others and relate to others. We cannot harbor anger, resentment, or hatred toward others and at the same time genuinely praise God. A negative spirit toward others and positive praise to God simply cannot coexist. God's command may compel us to move to a deeper level of commitment or to move out in a closer walk of faith.

We worship and praise the Lord to keep our attention on Him. When we're engaged in honoring God's worth and are spiritually open, we're much more likely to hear what He has to say to us.

You may begin your praise out of a sense of duty. You may come to God only out of obedience and begin praising Him without having a completely thankful heart. But once you start praising Him, you cannot continue for long without that negative spirit being broken. I have seen this happen over and over again in my own life. No matter how bleak or sad my circumstances, I am uplifted as I praise the Lord. As I honor God for who He is and for the glorious things He has done, my eyes are opened to His abundant provision and blessing.

Prepare your heart for praise and fix your attention on the Lord today so you can understand who He is and what He wants you to know and become.

⌒

Great and mighty God, whose name is the LORD Almighty, great are your purposes and mighty are your deeds. Your eyes are open to the ways of all mankind; you reward each person according to their conduct and as their deeds deserve.

JEREMIAH 32:18-19

Lord, You are infinitely good. You are infinitely great. Does my praise reflect how much I adore You? There are not adequate words to express the depth of my gratitude or the heights of my awe. When I seek Your mercy and sense Your forgiveness, I am moved by Your love to praise You. I want You to feel the love You show me reflected back to You a hundred times over.

I seek You with faith. My attention is on You. My eyes are open to see You. My ears are open to hear You. My mind is open to all You teach me. My spirit is open to receive You. And it's my prayer that You will always know my praise comes from a sincere, grateful, and open heart. All You are draws me closer as our fellowship grows sweeter. There is nothing better, Lord. Amen.

(50)

FULL SURRENDER

On days when our heart is just not into the act of praise, it's possible to fool others and even to fool ourselves, but it's never possible to fool God. He knows the intent, motives, and desires of our heart. For praise to be acceptable to almighty God, our heart must be true. And when the Bible speaks of the heart, it means the totality of our inner being—the intricate combination of intellect, emotional response, and will. All three of these must line up with God's perfect will.

You may think, *Well, then I don't have a chance! My intellect, emotions, and will often move in the opposite direction from God's plan.* My friend, don't be dismayed. God never intended for you to conform to His will on your own. That's why He sent His Holy Spirit to give you the power to live a righteous life. That's the very essence of His grace.

God has never made a demand on us that He hasn't covered by His own provision. His Holy Spirit nudges, prods, molds, and fashions us so that our heart is true—so that our thoughts line up with our words, our words line up with our behavior, and our motives and plans line up with God's desires. Total surrender.

In Genesis 22 we find a wonderful picture of a believer's total submission to God. It's the account of Abraham's response when the Lord commanded him to offer his son Isaac as a burnt offering.

Abraham submitted his intellect when he obeyed this command. He surrendered his heart and his feelings as well to bind his son to an altar and to raise a knife against him. It was a full surrender of his will to follow God's will. And he did it because he fully expected God to raise Isaac from the dead. Abraham knew that the Lord would stand by His promise to bless the earth through Isaac.

The decision to surrender all your life before God is an individual decision. Abraham did not even tell his wife, Sarah, what God had commanded. I have wondered what I would do in such a situation. Would I be willing to obey without first gathering Christian brothers around me to offer their prayers and advice? I feel certain that if Abraham had consulted anyone else, he would have been told, in so many words, "Abe, you're not thinking clearly. Surely God doesn't want you to do this. You're hearing a voice, all right, but it's not God's."

I am not at all suggesting that it is wrong to ask for godly counsel. But in the end, we are personally responsible for surrendering fully to God. We must obey as He directs us. God expects our surrender to be total, to be daily, and to be a sacrifice.

In this way, praise costs us something—our pride and our self-serving plans. Pride is deadly, which is why we need the healing and protection that come through the praise of our Lord. Praise reveals pride for the spiritual disease that it is. Either pride will stop the flow of praise from a person's lips, or praise will uproot and defeat pride. But pride isn't the only sin that kills praise. An untrue heart—insincere, hypocritical, or filled with doubt—can also squelch both our desire and our ability to praise God.

Praise requires that we lay ourselves down on an altar before the Lord and say, "I yield to You every aspect of my life—all my talents, all my possessions, all my dreams, all my relationships." This full surrender is an act that only a sincere, faithful heart can manage. Otherwise, we try to hold on to our wishes, desires, and plans—our autonomy.

God dwells in your praise, my friend. There is only room when all of you has been surrendered to all of Him.

Praise and exalt and glorify the King of heaven, because everything he does is right and all his ways are just. And those who walk in pride he is able to humble.

DANIEL 4:37

Lord Jesus, You know my heart and my intentions. Help me to recognize anything I have been holding on to that You have asked me to surrender. Reveal to me my points of pride and anything I am keeping between myself and Your heart. I want intimacy with You. Show me what it looks like to surrender my intellect, my emotions, my talents, and my will so all can be used for Your glory and purposes. You transform what I give to You into something beyond what I could imagine.

Abraham's faithfulness was a personal act of devotion. He knew that being obedient to You was between You and him alone. Help me to surrender and obey You daily so that I may worship You in this intimate way. My offering to You is all of me. May my wholehearted sacrifice be pleasing to You and used for Your good. Amen.

51

GOD OF THE NOT ENOUGH

If you've ever held back from expressing prayer or praise because you didn't feel worthy of approaching God, please know that all who have put their trust in Jesus Christ can draw near to God's throne with confidence. If you try to come on your own merits, you won't have confidence that your prayers will be heard, but if you come trusting in nothing but what Jesus has done for you, then you will find grace in times of need.

We live in a culture where there is a lot of exploration about people's "not enough" syndrome. Glance at social media or engage in conversation with a few folks, and this will come up. And as one person states this sentiment, there are dozens more who chime in to tell that person they are unequivocally enough. Of course we are dear to God. We have value as His children! However, there is a truth beneath the "not enough" mindset because we are not enough except for the power of God in us, His grace over us, and His love flowing through us.

In addition to verbally expressing our thanks to God, one of the best ways we can demonstrate our gratitude is through our giving. And it's no surprise that many of us can feel as though we are not enough when it comes to what we offer and how we give.

Jesus said, "Where your money is, there you will find your heart" (Matthew

6:21, author's paraphrase). Note that He did not single out preaching or teaching or any other highly visible ministry involvement as the primary indicator of the spiritual health of your heart. Instead, He made it clear that how you spend your money demonstrates where your heart is.

When Jesus told the story of the widow's mite—found in Luke 21:1-4—He commended the woman's generosity because He could see her heart. She gave out of her poverty, and she gave sacrificially. Her meager gift meant more to her, and to the Lord, because it was given out of scarcity.

And yet she may have felt her offering was not enough. She may have regretted that she was not able to give more, though she barely had enough money to cover basic needs. She waited until others dispersed their gifts before she gave her small offering. But Jesus was still there, and He noted the woman's generosity.

If you have ever felt you weren't enough to come to God because of your background, random prayer life, or brokenness, the most important thing for you to do is go to Him. He is enough. His enough covers your lack. The throne of grace represents the seat of God's unmerited favor and kindness toward us. The throne signifies His unlimited forgiveness and the blessings, power, and strength He extends to us. If you are distraught and fearful, or confused and anxious, there is comfort, wisdom, and discernment for you at the throne of grace. If you are discouraged and about to give up, there is encouragement for you at the throne of grace. If you are weak and defeated, there is victory for you at the throne of grace.

James wrote, "You do not have because you do not ask God" (James 4:2). When we begin to understand God's awesome grace and mercy, running to the throne of grace will become a regular habit. God has promised that we will find help. And when we make prayer and praise the pattern of our lives, we will learn to extend the comfort and strength we find to others who are struggling. When your heart is right with God and your intentions are pure, *you are enough* and your offering of praise, prayer, or money is enough.

~~~~~~~~

As Jesus looked up, he saw the rich putting their gifts into the temple treasury. He also saw a poor widow put in two very small copper coins. "Truly I tell you," he said, "this poor widow has put in more than all the others."

Luke 21:1-3

God, I have felt that I wasn't enough. A setback or stumble will cause me to doubt everything I know about my worth. To make up for my lack, I try to elevate my value with words and actions. I strive for perfection so nobody can question that I deserve a place at the table, a voice in the conversation. When in Your presence, even, I put on my "Sunday best" attitude so my requests and praises might be deemed worthy.

Turn my eyes from the external to the eternal, Lord. I look to You and know Your loving eyes are on me, Your ears are open to my cry and my praise, and Your heart receives my sincere, humble offering with delight. I praise You today. In You my value remains constant because Your grace alone— not my effort—saves me and makes me worthy. Amen.

52

THE GIVING SPIRIT

When you experience a time of feasting in your life and you give God the crumbs off your plate, that doesn't honor Him. But when you're facing the possibility of famine and make a sacrificial gift, you are honoring God (like the widow who gave the small coins). When everything is falling apart and you give sacrificially, you are learning the grace of giving.

The normal human reaction when we're going through trials is to ignore the suffering of others. We're tempted to think, *I can barely pay my own bills. I just can't help anybody else.* Recalling the widow at the temple, however, we realize this is not the attitude of those who have freely received the grace of God. Grace-givers understand that problems are simply a part of life. They should have no bearing on our giving.

In times of difficulty, grace-givers become more sensitive to the pain of others, more patient with those who are struggling, more willing to help financially. Grace-givers allow their trials to move them to minister to others with compassion.

The grace of giving is never an obligation, like paying income taxes. If you view giving to God as a burden or an obligation, then you are missing out on the overflowing joy that comes from being a "hilarious" giver (see 2 Corinthians 9:7). The word often translated "cheerful" in this verse is the Greek word *hilaros*, which has the connotation of exuberance and merriment. Grace giving is hilarious giving, and it's those who give with hilarity whom God loves.

The amount of our gifts may be small but can appear large in the eyes of God when they are given sacrificially. In addition, the sacrifice must be made freely. Grace-givers learn to be hilarious-givers, and in return they receive an outpouring of God's blessings. When you follow the example of hilarious giving, all your needs will be met, and you will have adequate resources to continue investing in God's work.

As we shine a light on praising God as our refuge and strength, it's valuable and transformative to consider how our giving spirit permeates not only how we give of our money and time to God's purposes and to others, but also how we give praise to the One responsible for our every blessing. When life is hard, can you give praise like the widow gave money—in a wholehearted, good intentioned, and sacrificial way?

And when you are feasting on blessing after blessing, do you also rush to God to thank Him and praise Him for all that is being poured into your life?

Living in grace and giving in grace go hand in hand. Those who have received much must give much as an expression of gratitude to God. Indeed, generous giving is an unseen source of contentment even amid trials.

In 2 Corinthians 8:1-5, we read that, out of their most severe trial, the Macedonian Christians overflowed with joy, and they expressed that joy by giving. What could have made them joyful when they were facing such severe trials? They took joy in the fact that God's grace had found them, and they had been brought out of the darkness of paganism into the light of Christ. The joy of their salvation overflowed into the joy of giving.

Is this a time of plenty for you? Or is it a season of limited resources and trials? Consider whether this has changed the way you come to the Lord in praise. We looked at how you are enough when you are in God and saved in Christ. That is established. Now the question becomes, Is your praise enough?

Is it overflowing and sacrificial? Follow your heart to the foot of the cross, and let that praise flow from a place of unlimited gratitude and joy.

You will be enriched in every way so that you can be generous on every occasion, and through us your generosity will result in thanksgiving to God.

2 Corinthians 9:11

Father, at times I struggle to give willingly of my resources and of my heart. I want to be a grace-giver and also a gracious giver who is not tallying what I give here and there, including my praise. I desire to pour my praise out to You without limits or expectations.

I never want to be a frugal, calculating believer. May I turn to You with songs of praise from a sincere heart whether in the midst of a trial or the midst of a triumph. Times of plenty will come and so will times of want. These scenarios don't indicate Your faithfulness. Your faithfulness is evident by Your presence and mercy during all seasons. Today I express my deep love for You and Your generosity. You are forever my refuge and strength, and I praise You with a giving heart that is inspired by Your grace and goodness. Amen.

53

GOD'S POWER ACTIVATED

Did you realize that your praise activates God's power in your life? Nowhere is this more evident than in the realm of spiritual warfare. Praise speaks the truth about God, something the devil cannot stand to hear. So the more you praise God's nature and love, His mercy and forgiveness, His refuge and strength, the less Satan can get away with his lies.

Satan is "the foe and the avenger," to use David's words from Psalm 8:2, and in praising God we proclaim His victory over this enemy. It's no accident that this psalm begins with David's proclamation of praise: "LORD, our Lord, how majestic is your name in all the earth!" (Psalm 8:1). Then David goes on to say, "Through the praise of children and infants you have established a stronghold against your enemies, to silence the foe and the avenger" (Psalm 8:2).

David may well have written this after defeating Goliath, the giant who sought to avenge the Philistines' previous defeats at the hands of Israel. Satan seeks a similar vengeance today. He lost the spiritual war at Calvary and has been seeking vengeance on believers ever since. He tries to enslave our bodies and take over our minds with paralyzing doubts and fears. He floods our spirits with guilt and shame and steals our joy as he undermines our relationship with Christ Jesus and His church.

The story of David and Goliath foreshadows the ultimate spiritual battle waged a thousand years later between Christ and Satan. In fact, David's defeat of Goliath is a model for our spiritual warfare today. Just as Goliath mocked and taunted the Israelites (see 1 Samuel 17), so Satan mocks and taunts us today. Will we stand up in indignation and righteousness, as David did? Or will we cower in fear, just as King Saul and the rest of the Israelite army did?

We may not battle giants when we're out running errands, but many of us encounter people or ideologies that challenge our beliefs. When the Pharisees rebuked Jesus during His triumphant entry into Jerusalem, He quoted to them David's praise for God in Psalm 8 that we just looked at—"From the lips of children and infants you, Lord, have called forth your praise" (Matthew 21:16). What did Jesus mean? And what did David mean when he first sang this same sentiment?

Think for a moment about the faith of a young child. A child doesn't have doubts about whether God can do certain things. A child simply loves and believes and hopes. And so must we. The great strength of our praise in spiritual warfare is that by it we declare with childlike faith that God loves us and has gained the victory over Satan. God loves and God wins. Period.

When you're faced with a spiritual struggle—discouragement or temptation, fear, or doubt—the best course of action is to exalt the position of God as the great victor in the battle against Satan. Praise God for sending Jesus to win the eternal war over your soul. Praising God will make the difference between winning or losing in every spiritual conflict you encounter.

Satan ultimately lost in his showdown with Jesus at the cross. God secured our salvation through Christ, and that is our power against Satan's attacks. Praise God, therefore, for raising Jesus from the dead so that you have the hope of eternal life. Praise Him because you heard the gospel, and because He convicted you of your sinful nature by the power of His Holy Spirit. Praise Him because He loves you enough to lead you daily so you might be conformed to the image of Christ.

Amid the darkness of spiritual warfare, praise God with the faith of a child because you'll live in the light of His glory for all eternity.

⌁

Shout for joy to God, all the earth!
    Sing the glory of his name;
    make his praise glorious.
Say to God, "How awesome are your deeds!
    So great is your power
    that your enemies cringe before you."

PSALM 66:1-3

God, I am reminded today of the blessing of spiritual protection under Your power. I can walk in confident faith because the battle is won through Christ. I won't remain stuck in my transgressions because You receive my offerings of confession and praise, and You redeem me. When I feel as though the world is against me and no one is for me, I know in my spirit this isn't true. You surround me with Your love and guide me with Your wisdom. I abide in You and find hope, renewal, and even joy.

I have a future because my salvation is secured in Jesus. With this truth, I am emboldened by Your power to take on whatever comes. I won't face my circumstances with an attitude of defeat but one of victory. With the trust and faith of a child, I know I am loved by You forever. Amen.

54

YOUR EMPOWERED PRAYERS

We strengthen our muscles by lifting weights and being faithful in our repetitions. We strengthen our prayers by lifting praises and being faithful in our repetition of going to God. In time, the practice of praise builds up our faith so that when we make our petitions before God, we pray with expectancy and confidence that we will receive God's best.

Consider the person who praises God, saying: "You are mighty, O Lord. You have made heaven and Earth. You're the Author and Finisher of all faith, the Creator and Sustainer of all that is good. You are almighty God." How can a person who praises the Lord in that way then pray, "God, I hope You'll meet my need"?

Our empowered faith puts us in a position to pray, "All things are possible for my God." That was the mindset of the apostle Paul when he wrote from a prison cell, "I can do all this through him who gives me strength" (Philippians 4:13).

The more we praise God, the more we realize that not only does He know about our needs, but He also desires to provide all that we need. God wants us to ask Him to meet our needs not so that He'll become better informed about them, but so that we will become more aware of what is truly burdening us and tugging at our hearts. And so that we will become more aware that He is ultimately our strength for everything.

Praise expressed in words like the following, puts us in a position to receive answers from God:

- You are all-powerful, Father. You can do all things.

- You are all-merciful to Your children, Father. You desire to bless us in all ways.

- You are patient and forgiving, Father. You long to draw all Your children close to You.

By giving God such praise, we realize that He is already supremely concerned about and fully capable of handling any petition we could ever make.

But how can we know if our requests are within His will? We begin by finding in God's Word the promises God makes to all believers so that we can focus our prayers on them. Then we can make our petitions in light of the things that count for eternity. Remember that Jesus told His disciples to "seek first his kingdom and his righteousness, and all these things will be given to you as well" (Matthew 6:33).

Paul told the Ephesians that he was asking God to give them "the Spirit of wisdom and revelation, so that you may know him better" (Ephesians 1:17). Our desire to seek God's kingdom first and to come to the Lord first with our needs is precisely what helps us know and trust His nature and character. This leads us back to praise!

Certainly, the Lord desires to meet our practical needs, and we aren't condemned by God when we mention them. But when we redirect our petitions to those things that involve spiritual wholeness and deliverance from evil, we grow in faith and develop spiritual maturity. Those who pray with faith will see God break the strongholds of the enemy and the shackles of our difficulties. It takes faith to confess that your body is the temple of the Holy Spirit who lives in you and works through you. It takes faith to stand against the enemy of your mind and body.

Because the assault against us is spiritual, our weapons of praise and prayer are also spiritual. When our faith is founded on the goodness and power of our mighty and unconquerable Savior and Lord, our faith is likewise mighty and unconquerable.

Commit to getting into shape. Build your faith and lift those praises daily. You will strengthen what matters most in your daily battles and your spiritual journey.

You are my strength, I sing praise to you;
    you, God, are my fortress,
    my God on whom I can rely.

Psalm 59:17

Lord, I have worked in my own power for so long. I am weary. Depleted. Unsure of how I can press on. But You offer Your strength to me, and I am grateful. It's time for me to lift my praises and build my faith, to be empowered for this human life and my spiritual journey. I want a spirit that is emboldened by Your Word and able to stand strong when I encounter challenges, obstacles, and times of doubt.

You are mighty and all-powerful, yet You don't keep that power to Yourself. What a gift that I can seek it and have it in me. Even in the toughest times, You are with me. I can lift my praises and know that I am infused by that power to do good work, to speak Your truth, and to build the strength of others with Your promises. Amen.

(55)

GOD'S LOVE

The more we praise God for who He is, the more awesome He becomes in our understanding. And with that awareness, in time we might start to question why this holy, perfect, all-wise God would care about each of us. Why should He care about me?

There's no explanation for why God desires to be in relationship with you other than this one truth: He loves you unconditionally. There isn't anything you have done to warrant His love. It truly is a free and undeserved gift from God. Many people engage in countless good works to try to earn enough points to win God's love. They don't realize they already have His love and His attention. They have the promise of His salvation held out to them with the open arms of Jesus on the cross.

What motivated Jesus to come to earth to die an agonizing death so that you might be spared the eternal consequences of your sin? What motivated Him to then send the Holy Spirit to seal your belief in Him? There is only one answer: love.

Everything Jesus did on Earth was a reflection of God's love, giving us a picture of that love in terms we can understand. Jesus hugged little children, dealt tenderly with those who confessed their sins, healed the sick, gave hope to the downtrodden, delivered those who were oppressed and possessed by demons, and set free those who were trapped by shame and guilt. In Jesus, we see love. And Jesus said, "Anyone who has seen me has seen the Father" (John 14:9).

How do you live differently knowing you are loved unconditionally by God? Does reading about the love of Jesus and experiencing it as a believer change the way you approach your days, life, vocation, tasks, trials, and relationships? Consider whether you show up in the world with joy inside of you because you are His child.

If you sense that the truth of His love is not fully influencing your behavior, hopes, actions, words, and thoughts, pause to consider why. What holds you back from fully accepting His love and allowing it to transform you in every way? Do echoes of your past before you knew the Lord make you doubt whether anything has changed? I assure you that everything has changed, and I encourage you to praise God for His love right now. Thank Him for words of encouragement you received recently or for a time when you felt the warmth of His presence. Lean into His love. Let it fill your speech and the way you interact with others. Let it change you inside and out, my friend.

Trusting this love and God's faithfulness becomes a mark of our faith. Saying we trust God and praising Him when things are going well is one thing. Actually trusting God's provision and praising Him even before we see evidence of His intervention or before circumstances change is an entirely different act of faith.

When Peter and John were arrested for healing a lame man outside the temple in Jerusalem, the authorities warned them never to preach about Jesus again. John and Peter went back and reported this to the other believers. Rather than cower in fear, they raised their voices in praise and bold prayer. They trusted God and were confident in His love and purpose.

The apostle John told how he knew that God is love:

> This is how God showed his love among us: He sent his one and
> only Son into the world that we might live through him. This is

love: not that we loved God, but that he loved us and sent his Son as an atoning sacrifice for our sins (1 John 4:9-10).

Praise God today for His infinite, sacrificial love…an unconditional love that flows with mercy, forgiveness, and grace.

Since we are surrounded by such a great cloud of witnesses, let us throw off everything that hinders and the sin that so easily entangles. And let us run with perseverance the race marked out for us, fixing our eyes on Jesus, the pioneer and perfecter of faith. For the joy set before him he endured the cross, scorning its shame, and sat down at the right hand of the throne of God.

Hebrews 12:1-2

Father, some days I struggle to fully accept how much You love me. I know of Your love and certainly I have felt it, but my heart still questions it when I am feeling undeserving. Forgive me, Lord. When I hesitate to believe, it's because I have shifted my focus from Your perfect love to my imperfect human love. This disbelief recedes in the light of what I know to be true—in love, You sacrificed for my salvation; in love, You sent the Holy Spirit; and in love, You desire relationship with me.

Thank You, God, for all You do to nurture my faith even after I have doubted. I praise You, Jesus, as the Author and Perfecter of my faith, and I praise You, Holy Spirit, for testifying within my spirit that I am a child of God. I cling to this truth that I am Your beloved. Amen.

56

PRAISE HIS NAME

Praise the name of the Lord! Throughout the book of Psalms we read this admonition, and we hear it frequently in the church as well. But what does it mean to praise the Lord's name? Shouldn't we concentrate instead on what God does?

The names of God revealed in Scripture are not a human invention. They are the way in which God has chosen to reveal His character to us. The names of God are a composite of God's revelation of His nature, His identity, His sovereignty, and His desires. If you want to know God, get to know His names. The names of God are evidence that He desires for us to know Him intimately, to praise Him completely, and to enter more fully into a deep and abiding relationship with Him.

Many churches on Sunday morning sing an upbeat Scripture chorus that speaks of bringing a sacrifice of praise into the house of the Lord. The basis for this is in Hebrews 13:15: "Through Jesus, therefore, let us continually offer to God a sacrifice of praise—the fruit of lips that openly confess his name." A sacrifice of praise is the confession of the names of the Lord—it's speaking His name in relationship to our personal life.

When we praise the Lord using the names of God, we are praising the Trinity, the full Godhead, because God's Old Testament names are not reserved only for the Father. They reveal the nature of the triune God—Father, Son, and Holy Spirit.

Using the names of God allows us to praise Him in His fullness. In the next few devotions, we will look at some of these so you can discover the wonders of praising Him in this way. I hope you will discover a new and very personal and powerful way to speak with the Lord and enter into a deeper relationship with Him.

The first name God revealed to humanity was *Elohim*, a name that appears more than 2,500 times throughout the Old Testament. God's people knew that this name referred to the "most high" God or the "highest" God—the God above all creation, the God who initiated and created all of life.

Living all around God's people were pagans who worshipped gods they had fashioned and defined according to human standards. To declare that there was only one God and that He reigned supreme over the entire universe was a radically different concept.

When God's people encountered nations who worshipped Baal, the god of fertility, the Hebrews responded, "We worship *Elohim*, the One who authorizes the birth of children." When they encountered pagans who worshipped the god Shamish, the sun god, the Hebrews responded, "We worship *Elohim*. He is the One who put the sun in its place and who governs its course."

Elohim, the God of all creation, includes all three persons of the Trinity. I can't help but believe that anytime we really begin to praise our Father and His Son and the Holy Spirit with the many names of God, we'll grow in our awareness of His presence with us. The more we catch a glimpse of all that God does and who He is, the more we'll want to praise Him. The more we know God through praising Him by name, the more we'll see Him at work in our lives, and the more we'll experience manifestations of His presence and power.

As you begin to praise aloud the names of God, I believe a spirit of revival will flood your soul. You'll find yourself energized and renewed. You'll find your attitude growing more hopeful and your faith growing more powerful.

Praise *Elohim*! He is the one true and living God. He is the Creator of each new day in your life, each new experience you encounter, and each new spiritual work in you. He is the Author and Finisher of your faith.

I will be glad and rejoice in you;
    I will sing the praises of your name, O Most High.

PSALM 9:2

I praise You, God, for connecting with Your creation in personal ways. Your names bring to light aspects of who You are and how You relate to us, love us, and care for us. Today, I praise You as Elohim, *the Most High God. You are above all You have created. You are the one true God. I have experienced Your power in my life through my surrender to Your will. I am eager to have Your guidance as I step forward in my days in faith because there is no power above You.*

I will trust in You—Father, Son, and Holy Spirit—to do what pleases You from the heights of heaven to the depths of the sea and in my depths. What in me pleases You, Elohim? *As Your creation, I pray I will honor You and bring You delight, Most High God. Amen.*

57

PRAISE GOD ALMIGHTY

While you and I might admit that we make mistakes, we may not readily confess to the reason those mistakes are sometimes made—because
we're trying to do things in our own strength, without God. Even believers
stumble over the words "I can't do this on my own." Who can blame us? Self-
sufficiency is applauded in our culture and in our minds. It feels good when
we complete a home project on our own or figure out the fastest backroad
route to someplace without GPS.

But what happens when our personal "I can do all things" mindset filters
into areas of important decisions and spiritual matters? We miss having the
power of God Almighty, *El-Shaddai*, active in our lives. And we miss out on
what happens when God Almighty appears. Nearly every time God expresses
Himself as *El-Shaddai*, He indicates a change that will occur in that person's
life, a change that will involve a miraculous intervention.

To Abraham, who was then called Abram, God revealed more of His
nature when He revealed Himself as *El-Shaddai*. This name means "God of
power and might."

God said to Abram: "I am God Almighty [*El-Shaddai*]; walk before me
faithfully and be blameless. Then I will make my covenant between me and
you and will greatly increase your numbers" (Genesis 17:1-2). God told Abram
that he would have many descendants and that his name would be changed

to Abraham, which means "father of many nations." *El-Shaddai* was going to intervene and use His power to cause Abraham to father a son, even though Abraham's wife, Sarai, was barren.

God later used this same divine name when He revealed Himself to Jacob, saying, "I am God Almighty; be fruitful and increase in number. A nation and a community of nations will come from you, and kings will be among your descendants" (Genesis 35:11).

At the time God spoke these words, Jacob had lost his son Joseph and didn't know he was still alive in Egypt. God was saying to Jacob, in essence, "I am going to intervene on your behalf. You will become a great nation, and you will receive this land I have promised to you. I am the Lord Almighty—the course of nature and the course of history run according to My plans" (see Genesis 35:12).

God wants there to be no misunderstanding—as *El-Shaddai*, He is the ruler and owner of all things. He is the controlling force of all nature and all history. This name reveals a God who controls and subdues nature. We read of this power in an incredible story of Jesus on a boat with the disciples during a storm.

One evening after a long day of ministry, Jesus and His disciples were crossing the Sea of Galilee in a small boat, and a great storm arose. They were in danger of capsizing when the disciples finally woke Jesus, who was calmly asleep. They cried, "Teacher, don't you care if we drown?" (Mark 4:38).

"He got up, rebuked the wind, and said to the waves, 'Quiet! Be still!'" (Mark 4:39). The wind died down immediately, and the sea became calm. The disciples were awestruck and said to one another, "Who is this? Even the wind and the waves obey him!" (Mark 4:41).

The answer is that Jesus is *El-Shaddai*, God Almighty, who governs the winds and the waves and fulfills His plans on the earth.

What storm is brewing in your life right now? Do you need help seeing a way forward in an unexpected circumstance? Then cry out to *El-Shaddai*. Begin to praise God Almighty! He alone can hold you up when all seems to be crumbling around you. He alone can ride the clouds to bring help for you. He alone can open doors that no one can shut and shut doors that no one else can open.

He stilled the storm to a whisper;
　　the waves of the sea were hushed.
They were glad when it grew calm,
　　and he guided them to their desired haven.

PSALM 107:29-30

I praise You, El-Shaddai. You are mightier than all of nature and all of my efforts. There is nothing You can't do. I call out to You today to calm this storm that has brought upheaval to my life and relationships. There is chaos within me too. I might say I'm fine, but You know I need help. No amount of striving in my power is going to lead me to the peace of Your purpose.

Do Your work inside my heart. Change me. Change the conditions around me. Set me back on solid ground and show me the way to move forward. Your presence signals change is coming, and, honestly, I'm glad. I'm so tired of trying to accomplish everything in my limited strength. I surrender my will and my tight grip on this situation. Praise You, El-Shaddai, for bringing forth the winds of change and healing. Amen.

（58）

PRAISE OUR PROVIDER, OUR HEALER

Many cries from the hearts of believers are for provision and healing. Think back on your times of seeking God these past few weeks or months. Did you ask God to provide a way, a hope, the fulfillment of a basic need? Did you bring your brokenness to Him with a prayer for help and healing?

In those times, you were seeking comfort and mercy from God as *Jehovah-Jireh* and *Jehovah-Rapha*, the names which mean our Provider and our Healer.

Jehovah is an English rendition of the Hebrew *Yahweh*, the name for God that is used in the Old Testament more than any other—more than 6,800 times (in English Bibles it's usually translated as "the LORD"). This name literally means "to be." It has been translated as "the Self Existing One." Our God depends upon nothing and no one for His existence.

One of the foremost variations of this name is *Jehovah-Jireh*, which means "the Lord will provide." It's the name Abraham used for the place on the mountain where God had sent him to sacrifice his beloved son Isaac as a burnt offering depicted in Genesis 22.

On the way up this mountain, Isaac said to his father, "'Where is the lamb for the burnt offering?' Abraham answered, 'God himself will provide the lamb for the burnt offering, my son'" (Genesis 22:7-8).

As you may know from this story of obedience and faithfulness, Abraham was about to sacrifice his son as he was told to do when the angel of the Lord said, "Do not lay a hand on the boy...Now I know that you fear God, because you have not withheld from me your son, your only son" (Genesis 22:12). Then Abraham saw a ram caught by its horns in a nearby thicket. He took the ram and sacrificed it in place of his son. And he called that place *Jehovah-Jireh*, "The LORD Will Provide" (Genesis 22:14).

The word *jireh* literally means "he sees ahead." God knows our need before we do. For every task or burden God gives you, He has already made full provision for all you'll need to face it, complete it, and endure it with peace.

This is also true when our need is healing and wholeness. This is when we seek and praise our Healer. The word *rapha* means "to heal and to restore." God doesn't promise to heal us only in isolated instances. Rather, God says He is healing. He is our wholeness. He is the fulfillment of what we need, no matter what weakness or sickness or trouble we encounter.

Does this mean God isn't true to His name if a believer becomes ill or is suffering from a terminal disease? Not at all. That believer can be assured that God desires to use this suffering to bring an even greater reward of healing to that person and to bring a greater awareness of His healing presence to others who may witness the person's steadfastness.

God tells us He will never forsake us, not even in death. He's with us always, working all things to our eternal good. In the moment of our death, God seals the wholeness issue, and we truly are made whole for all eternity.

The ongoing work of the Holy Spirit in our world is the work of *Jehovah-Rapha*. It's the Holy Spirit who mends broken hearts, renews degenerate minds, restores shattered relationships, and heals disease. It's the work of the Holy Spirit to conform us to the likeness of the perfect, complete Christ Jesus.

Praise *Jehovah-Jireh* and *Jehovah-Rapha*. When you come to God and praise His names, you stand in His presence and become a part of the history of

God's people seeking His help. Praise your God who sees ahead and already has a plan to provide everything you'll ever need and who makes you whole.

⌒

They cried to the LORD in their trouble,
   and he saved them from their distress.
He brought them out of darkness, the utter darkness,
   and broke away their chains.
Let them give thanks to the LORD for his unfailing love
   and his wonderful deeds for mankind.

PSALM 107:13-15

God, You are my provider and healer. Before I even know what I will need, You have created a plan to fulfill that need. When I look about for help and forget to come to You with my pain, my burdens, and even my hope, forgive me. You are my source of help. I praise You, Jehovah-Jireh, for Your perfect provision. I will wait patiently and with faith for Your well-timed provision because You see ahead and know precisely what is needed to bring light to darkness and glory to Your name.

Jehovah-Rapha, You are the healing and wholeness I desire. You do not leave Your children to languish and struggle. When I am hurting, You are there providing comfort. You whisper to my heart a reminder that You are making me whole for eternity. God, Your names lead me to Your nature. I sing Your praises because You alone are God. Amen.

PRAISE OUR SHEPHERD, OUR PEACE

If decision fatigue is a part of your life the way it is mine, I can imagine the relief you would feel if someone else made the choices or led the way now and then. Forging a path through our daily existence can be exhausting. In God's Word, He provides us with a beautiful image of a shepherd leading, protecting, and caring for his sheep. *Rohi* is the Hebrew word for "shepherd," and there's no more tender word to describe the relationship between God and His people. This is the picture of God we see in Psalm 23, which begins, "The LORD is my shepherd; I shall not want" (NKJV).

Believers and even those who do not yet know the Lord personally seek this psalm to read of God as shepherd when they encounter a valley of trial or day after day of hard decisions. We are born with a heart that longs for His care. *Jehovah-Rohi*, God our Shepherd, provides for all our needs so we're never in want. Just as a shepherd leads his sheep to pasture, so the Lord leads us into places of abundant nourishment and rest, and into times of spiritual refreshment and retreat.

Jehovah-Rohi guides us into right decisions, beliefs, words, and actions. He never leaves us, and He is present when danger comes. He drives fear from us so we can do great works in His name. We can praise Him because His desire is for us to walk daily in His tender care and say, "Surely your goodness and love will follow me all the days of my life, and I will dwell in the house of the Lord forever" (Psalm 23:6).

God leads us as a gentle, protective shepherd. When we long to experience His peace, we can call out to Him as *Jehovah-Shalom*. In the Bible, we encounter Him in the book of Judges. The Israelites had been living under the tyranny of the Midianites, who routinely destroyed their crops and took or killed their livestock.

The Israelites had forgotten about God, but now they cried out for His help. He responded by sending the angel of the Lord to speak to Gideon. After Gideon realized who this visitor was, he exclaimed, "Alas, Sovereign Lord! I have seen the angel of the Lord face to face!" (Judges 6:22). Gideon held to the belief of his day that to have a direct encounter with the Lord was to die.

"But the Lord said to him, 'Peace! Do not be afraid. You are not going to die'" (Judges 6:23). Still today, those who have a face-to-face encounter with God and yield to His will, bowing before Him in repentance and praise, will be those who live not only now but forever.

In response to this visitation from God, Gideon built an altar that he named *Jehovah-Shalom*, "The Lord Is Peace" (Judges 6:24). *Shalom*, the Hebrew word for "peace," means far more than an absence of conflict or an emotional feeling of contentment. *Shalom* means perfect well-being. It means to be filled with a comprehensive peace that surpasses our understanding.

The Lord brings calm to our souls and a peace that cannot be shaken by life's circumstances. He gives us the peace that all is well and that we're destined to enjoy an eternity in the glorious light of His countenance. The only way to experience this unwavering peace is to know with certainty that God has met us, forgiven us, received us, and given us the gift of eternal life. Jesus doesn't just give us peace; He is our peace.

Praise *Jehovah-Rohi* and *Jehovah-Shalom*, for He shepherds you and is watchful over your steps from the day you are born on through eternity. No matter what you face now or anticipate in the future, may you lift these names of God with gratitude for the goodness and peace that will follow you all of your days.

Even though I walk
    through the darkest valley,
I will fear no evil,
    for you are with me;
your rod and your staff,
    they comfort me.

PSALM 23:4

My Shepherd, I thank You for Your tender care. I call out to Jehovah-Rohi *and* Jehovah-Shalom, *and You lead me, protect me, and guide me through the rough terrain from fear to peace. I don't need to be anxious about my circumstances because You ward off my enemies, rescue me when I am lost, and provide me with rest and shelter. Strengthened and encouraged by Your constant presence and the sound of Your voice, I know I will make it through any difficulties.*

Lord, I believe You will faithfully fill me with Your peace and meet my every need. You lead me through the pastures of this earthly journey to the vast landscape of the heavens. I will sing songs of praise each step of the way, unafraid of what is ahead because You have carried me through all that lies behind me. Under Your watch, I am safe in Your care forevermore. Amen.

(60)

A LIFE OF PRAISE

What brings forth your praise? Is it the joy in a child's face? The blessing of comfort after a season of sorrow? The sense of Jesus's love and power in the middle of a hard day? If we have developed a spirit that is always watching, noticing, and grateful, there will be no end to the reasons to sing, shout, whisper, or pray our praises to our merciful God.

Consider whether you are living your faith with a spirit and attitude of praise. If we open our eyes and heart to God's presence, we fully experience His character, care, provision, guidance, healing, and promises. It's as though spiritual blinders have been removed—blinders that kept us thinking we're alone and that all we do, are, or become is either random or done in our human strength. Suddenly, we know God is with us and at work in us, and we can't help but praise the Most High God.

Abundant praise transforms us and our faith journeys. We welcome the work of the Holy Spirit, and apathy is replaced with a hunger to learn more about God and where His Word leads us. We want more of God. And we want to be more like Christ.

A life of flowing praise leads to effective, merciful witnessing to those who don't know God and to love-laden ministry to the needy. Why? Because when we faithfully exalt the goodness and forgiveness and protection of God, we realize we're the recipients of these blessings in His tender care and others see this too. We develop a growing desire to extend care to others and lead them to God so they also will receive His blessings.

When we focus on how wonderful it is to be called a child of God and recognize the awesome reality of our salvation, we're driven to lead others to Christ so they, too, might be saved. We want them to experience the security and comfort of a personal, powerful faith.

Throughout the Old Testament, to worship God was to serve Him by doing those things that were pleasing to Him—to offer the sacrifices of praise He desired, to make the sacrificial gifts He commanded, to engage in righteous living, and to meet the needs of widows and orphans and others in need. Worship was an outward action, not simply words that were spoken.

So, too, is our worship today. When we come away from a time of praise, we're to put our praise into action—using our hands and feet and voices to show others that we truly believe what we've said about God.

We say to Jesus, "You are God incarnate. You're our Savior. You died to pay the debt for our sin. You're the only way to a relationship with God. You are the Lord." When we walk away from praising Jesus, our next task is to live in such a way that we express those realities in our behavior, and we share those proclamations with someone who doesn't know Jesus as Savior or who is discouraged in his or her faith walk. Our ultimate expression of praise to God is a life of obedience to His written commandments and to the daily guidance of the Holy Spirit.

During our time together, by God's grace, we have come through restlessness and discontent, and instead of running away, we have run to the refuge of the Lord. We have found peace and healing through the strength of God's presence, promises, and undeniable love. This, my friend, has been a journey to a life of praise. Live it well in Him, with Him, and for His glory forever. Amen!

I will sing of the LORD's great love forever;
> with my mouth I will make your faithfulness known
> through all generations.
I will declare that your love stands firm forever,
> that you have established your faithfulness in heaven itself.

PSALM 89:1-2

Lord, my restless longing and search for meaning and healing have led me to You. This time in Your presence stirs in me a great desire to serve You. No longer do I view worship as something I do only on Sunday. I will glorify and worship You through action, service, compassion, and sharing about Your grace.

It is time to live out my praise and gratitude in real ways. I can be Your hands to those in need...Your heart to those who hurt. Help me to be a person of spiritual integrity whose honesty and humility shows others that You are the way of truth and love. Amen.